APPENDIX II

Constitution of a Legal Organization Named:
Christian Democratic Party (C.D.P.)

1. The aim of the 'Christian Democratic Party' shall be to assure to all inhabitants 'Freedom and well being in a self-ruling and peaceful Nyasaland'.

2. This aim shall be pursued by all its members only through lawful and just means, recognizing all natural human rights and adhering to Christian principles.

3. The Christian Democratic Party claims for all inhabitants of Nyasaland, as equal citizens, the same individual and social rights and duties.

4. The C.D.P. wants the people of Nyasaland to be free from all sorts of oppression, discrimination and intimidation and to enjoy well being and peace under truly Democratic Government.

5. The C.D.P. will, subject only to good order and morality in particular, assure to everybody freedom and the rights:

   (a) to think, speak and write according to one's personal conviction.
   (b) to believe, worship, act and live to one's religious creed.
   (c) to possess property, individual or in partnership according to law and justice.

6. The C.D.P. will work for the well being of all by promoting more individual social and economic development:

   (a) individual development by obtaining more facilities for higher education and technical training.
   (b) social development advocating friendly co-existence and fraternal co-operation with all, irrespective of colour, race or creed, basing promotion and remuneration only on ability and merit.
   (c) economic development to be obtained through:
   Better agricultural methods and better produce.
   More and bigger industries.
   Intensification of trade and commerce, higher skilled labour, harder work, and higher wages.

7. The C.D.P. assures peace to every inhabitant of good will in Nyasaland by way of justice and charity.

POLICYMAKING IN MEXICO

THEMATIC STUDIES IN LATIN AMERICA

Series editor: Gilbert W. Merkx, Director, *Latin American Institute, University of New Mexico*

THE POLITICAL ECONOMY OF REVOLUTIONARY
NICARAGUA
by Rose J. Spalding

WOMEN ON THE U.S.–MEXICO BORDER: RESPONSES TO
CHANGE
edited by Vicki L. Ruiz and Susan Tiano

THE JEWISH PRESENCE IN LATIN AMERICA
edited by Judith Laikin Elkin and Gilbert W. Merkx

POLICYMAKING IN MEXICO: FROM BOOM TO CRISIS
by Judith A. Teichman

LAND, POWER, AND POVERTY: AGRARIAN
TRANSFORMATION AND POLITICAL CONFLICT IN
CENTRAL AMERICA
by Charles D. Brockett

Additional titles in preparation

POLICYMAKING IN MEXICO

From Boom to Crisis

JUDITH A. TEICHMAN

Boston
ALLEN & UNWIN
London   Sydney   Wellington

Copyright © 1988 by Allen & Unwin, Inc.
All rights reserved.

Allen & Unwin, Inc.
8 Winchester Place, Winchester, MA 01890, USA.

Published by the Academic Division of
Unwin Hyman Ltd,
15–17 Broadwick Street, London W1V 1FP

Allen & Unwin Australia Pty Ltd,
8 Napier Street, North Sydney, NSW 2060, Australia

Allen & Unwin (New Zealand) Ltd, in association with the
Port Nicholson Press Ltd
60 Cambridge Terrace, Wellington, New Zealand

Library of Congress Cataloging-in-Publication Data

Teichman, Judith A., 1947–
   Policymaking in Mexico.
   (Thematic studies in Latin America)
   Bibliography: p.
   Includes index.
   1. Petroleum industry and trade——Government policy
   ——Mexico. 2. Mexico——Economic policy——1970–
   3. Banks and banking——Government ownership——Mexico.
I. Title.   II. Series.
HD9574.M6T45   1988   338.2'7282'0972   87–18704
ISBN 0–04–445033–8
ISBN 0–04–445049–4 (pbk.)

British Library Cataloguing in Publication Data

Teichman, Judith A.
   Policymaking in Mexico: from boom to
   crisis.——(Thematic studies in Latin
   America).
   1. Petroleum industry and trade——
   Government policy——Mexico 2. Mexico
   ——Economic policy——1970–
I. Title   II. Series
338.2'7282'0972   HD9574.M6

ISBN 0–04–445033–8
ISBN 0–04–445049–4 Pbk

Set in 10 on 12 point Palatino
by Phoenix Photosetting, Chatham
and printed in Great Britain by Billing and Son Ltd,
London and Worcester

Contents

Acknowledgments

This book has acquired many debts over the last seven years. Seed money from the University of Waterloo's Research Grant Program allowed me to begin preliminary research in Mexico. Two additional trips in 1982 and in 1984–1985 were funded by the Social Sciences and Humanities Research Council of Canada.

I would like to thank Dr. Jorge Padua of the Colegio de México, who, back in 1981, encouraged me to undertake this project. I owe a special debt of gratitude to Dr. Jaime Serra Puche, also of the Colegio, who contributed to this project in countless ways, among them facilitating my access to the Colegio de México's excellent library collection. Sally Mott, an economist and fellow Canadian resident in Mexico during the period of my field research, was extremely helpful in providing advice and in helping me to track down various research materials.

This book would not be what it is without the patience and trust of the numerous Mexican government officials who gave freely of their time to help me understand the Mexican political process. Their enthusiasm for this project, their willingness to reveal their experiences, fears, and hopes, contributed immeasurably to this work.

Back home, fellow members of the Mexico Working Group, based at York University's Centre for Research on Latin America and the Caribbean, furnished valuable comments on working papers as the project progressed. Judith Adler Hellman of York University provided a careful and insightful reading of the manuscript. Thanks are also due to Sam Lanfranco of York University and Jorge Nef of the University of Guelph for their comments on selected chapters. Any errors and omissions are, of course, my own.

A very special debt is owed to my husband, George Teichman, who persevered through the trials of single parenthood during my various research stints in Mexico and who never failed to provide encouragement and support.

1
Underdevelopment and State Policy

Perspectives on Underdevelopment and the Third World State

In the late 1960s the scholarly focus on the roots of poverty in Asia, Africa, and Latin America shifted from a preoccupation with internal factors to concern over the obstacles imposed by the operation of the world economy. The roots of this paradigmatic shift are found in the reformist publications of the United Nation's Economic Commission for Latin America, which laid the blame for Latin America's underdevelopment on deterioration in the terms of trade and called for strong state action to propel industrialization. Later *dependendista* formulations became increasingly radical; ever greater emphasis was placed upon the external constraints imposed by capital outflows and technological transfers. Perhaps the best-known proponent of the dependency perspective, André Gunder Frank, despairing of the ability of any elite group to lead capitalist development, predicted the demise of capitalism in Latin America and the imminence of socialist revolution.[1]

But the recovery of capitalist growth in Latin America, particu-

---

Methodological Note: Much of the data in this book concerning the motivations and objectives of state managers was obtained from twenty-one open-ended interviews carried out in the fall of 1984 and the winter of 1985. As a pledge of confidentiality was a condition of all interviews no sources will be cited for the material obtained in this manner.

1 See for example, one of André Gunder Frank's earliest and best-known works, *Capitalism and Underdevelopment in Latin America* (New York: Modern Reader Paperbacks, 1969). T. Dos Santos was another radical scholar sharing Gunder Frank's view that socialist revolution was the only viable solution in Latin America. See 'The New Dependence,' in K. T. Fann and Donald C. Hodges, eds., *Readings in U.S. Imperialism* (Boston: Porter Sargent, 1971).

larly the 'Brazilian miracle' of 1968–1973, precipitated a reevaluation of the dependency perspective, especially in its more radical manifestations. It became clear that capitalist growth, albeit with increasing inequalities, could continue in the Third World. Dissident dependendista and Marxist critiques argued that the dependency perspective had disregarded internal factors, in particular the level of class conflict and the role of the state.[2] This recognition of the importance of internal political factors has since spawned studies examining the role of the Third World state in economic development, with special emphasis on its relations to domestic and international capital.[3]

Regardless of the specifics of the economic or political system, the Third World state has played a central and critical role in the direction of economic change. Its role has been qualitatively different and more extensive than that which has occurred in developed capitalist countries. The Third World state has expanded its activities through state enterprises—known as parastates—beyond the traditional areas of infrastructure and failing industries into areas such as minerals, petroleum, steel, and arms manufacture. In many countries of the Third World, state enterprises now constitute more than half of total investment.[4] The Third World state has also been an important source of development financing through state development banks.

The centrality of the Third World state is usually explained in terms of the failure of these countries to develop a large, independent, and hegemonic bourgeoisie due to colonial and neocolonial dominance. It has been suggested that the relative political and economic weakness of the national bourgeoisie (or its almost total absence) has propelled the state into an economic leadership role.

2 Some of the earliest examples include Ernesto Laclau, 'Feudalism and Capitalism in Latin America,' *New Left Review* 67 (1971); Fernando Henrique Cardoso, 'Las contradicciones del desarrollo asociado,' *Desarrollo económico* 14, núm. 53 (Abril–Junio 1974); Colin Leys, 'Underdevelopment and Dependency: Critical Notes,' *Journal of Contemporary Asia* 7, no. 1 (1977).

3 For a review of some of the most recent studies, see Peter Evans, 'After Dependency: Recent Studies of Class, State, and Industrialization,' *Latin American Research Review* 20, no. 2 (1985).

4 F. H. Cardoso, 'Capitalist Development and the State: Bases and Alternatives,' in E. V. K. Fitzgerald et al., eds., *The State and Economic Development in Latin America*, Occasional Paper No. 1, Center of Latin America Studies, University of Cambridge (Cambridge: University Publishing House, 1977), p. 15.

It has also been suggested that weak and evenly matched propertied classes—some of which may be precapitalist remnants—produce a hegemonic crisis that further strengthens the state.[5] The state, then, performs the role of mediating the interests of these various propertied classes rather than of organizing the hegemony of a single class as it is assumed occurs in advanced capitalist countries. But aside from the fact that these explanations account neither for the centrality of the state in areas of the Third World not subjected to colonialism nor for the weak and fractured state Latin America inherited as part of its colonial legacy, they also fail to account for the very marked increase in state intervention that has occurred in Third World countries over the past decade.[6]

Moreover, while the centrality of the Third World state is generally accepted, observers have disagreed sharply on the extent of the state's autonomy from domestic and international pressures and on its ability to transform society. Some have viewed the Third World state as largely the instrument of an alliance of multinational and domestic capital often operating under enormous geopolitical constraints as well.[7] Most, however, are willing to grant the Third World state a considerable degree of 'relative' autonomy, at least at certain historical junctures when the constraints imposed by the operation of capitalism recede. Indeed, the Third World state may even be capable of manipulating geopolitical factors in order to pursue a more independent development strategy.[8] The Third World state has been described

5 See, for example, Hamza Alavi, 'The State in Post-Colonial Societies: Pakistan and Bangladesh,' in Harry Goulbourne, ed., *Politics in the Third World* (London: Macmillan, 1979); Thomas Bamat, 'Relative State Autonomy and Capitalism in Brazil and Peru,' *The Insurgent Sociologist* 7, no. 2 (Spring 1977): 77; Norbert Lechner, 'La crisis del estado en América Latina,' *Revista mexicana de sociología* 39, núm 2 (Abril–Junio 1977): 400.

6 On East Africa, see Colin Leys, 'The Overdeveloped Post-Colonial State: A Reevaluation,' *Review of African Political Economy*, no. 5 (January–April 1976): 76. Also see Ben Turkok, 'Zambia's System of State Capitalism,' in *Development and Change* 11, no. 3 (July 1980): 459; and W. Ziemann and M. Lanzendörfer, 'The State in Peripheral Societies,' *The Sociologist Register* (1977): 144.

7 Perhaps the best-known example of this viewpoint is found in André Gunder Frank, *Lumpenbourgeoisie, Lumpendevelopment* (New York: Monthly Review Press, 1972) and *Crisis in the Third World* (New York: Holmes & Meier, 1981).

8 See, for example, Sanjib Basie, 'Nonalignment and Economic Development: Indian State Strategies, 1947–1962,' in Peter Evans et al., eds., *State versus Markets in the World System* (Newbury Park, CA: Sage Publications, 1985).

as having an 'extreme' or 'hyper' degree of relative autonomy. The Gramscian notion of 'exceptional state,' a form of state that occurs during periods of transition or during critical periods, is seen as particularly applicable to Third World countries.[9]

The high degree of relative autonomy of which the Third World state is supposedly capable enables it, it is assumed, to take those measures necessary both to preserve the social and political order and to perpetuate dependent capitalism.[10] It is readily acknowledged, however, that this is a far more formidable task than has been the case in the developed capitalist countries. In particular, lack of adequate resources makes it difficult to ensure the support of the popular sectors through social welfare measures. Hence, there is a tendency to resort to authoritarian political forms, a tendency that is reinforced by the greater relative strength of the state vis-à-vis society's most important social groups. The problem of maintaining legitimacy has resulted in what one author has called the 'predominance of the political,' reflecting the fact

9 During such periods the state apparatus is concentrated vertically—an extreme solution for moments of imminent crisis. There are two types of exceptional state. The Bonapartist state, as it has been applied to the Third World, corresponds to the populist state and is characterized by state autonomy achieved through state mobilization of the masses at a time when there is an equilibrium of power between the bourgeoisie and the masses. It has been suggested, however, that Bonapartism may be too restrictive a notion to be applied to Latin American populism because the social basis of such regimes is not clear and because they may not mediate class conflict. See David Raby, 'Populism: A Marxist Perspective,' *McGill Studies in International Development* No. 32. The other form of exceptional state is that of the highly repressive military regimes of the Southern cone of the late 1960s and early 1970s. Here a high degree of state autonomy stems from the failure of any class or faction among the propertied classes to achieve hegemony combined with a need to deal with a very strong threat from below from the popular classes. In this type, the state separates itself from any social basis and exercises fierce repression.

10 The terms *dependent* and *peripheral* capitalism are used interchangeably in the literature usually with little attempt at precise definition. Generally the terms connote the form of capitalism that exists in the countries of Asia, Africa, and Latin America. These countries, despite their admittedly wide diversity, are believed to share certain broad similarities: that of dependence on the exportation of primary products for the earning of foreign exchange; that of an unintegrated industrial structure; heavy dependence on imported machinery, equipment, and technology; and the increasing use of capital-intensive methods both in industry and agriculture, producing a large mass of an unemployed and underemployed population.

[4]

that the state is the focal point for conflict between capitalist factions and between capital and labor. The fact that the state must resolve these conflicts, he argues, means that it predominates over all areas of political life; that is, all disputes take place within definite boundaries set by the state.[11] Hence in Latin America, we have the emergence of the authoritarian corporatist state as the state attempts to establish a limited number of legally recognized groups that are obliged to interact with the state through designated leaders. The tension between strong social pressures and the state's effort to control them has led one observer to characterize the Latin American state as 'politicized,' a situation that further contributes to and is reinforced by the central role of the state, as groups, classes, and class fractions attempt to pressure the state to achieve their goals.[12]

Indeed, the apparent predominance of the Third World state in relation to the most important social groups, combined with its central role in directing development, has led to the claim that what has emerged or is emerging in many parts of the Third World is 'state capitalism' and a 'state bourgeoisie.' There is no clear agreement on the meaning of 'state capitalism.'[13] Most often the term 'state capitalism' is used to refer to a package of policies that include opposition to imperialism as demonstrated by nationalizations, state-led industrialization through the expansion of state enterprises, heavy state intervention in the economy, and perhaps some agrarian reform. The state bourgeoisie is usually conceived of as that group which is in charge of

11 Harry Goulbourne, 'Some Problems of Analysis of the Political in Backward Capitalist Countries,' in Harry Goulbourne, ed., *Politics and State in the Third World* (London: Macmillan, 1979), p. 26. On those occasions in which conflicts break out beyond the bounds set by the state, we have a situation of political chaos in which the response of the state is likely to be fierce repression as it strives to reestablish the limits of societal conflict.

12 Douglas A. Chalmers, 'The Politicized State in Latin America,' in James M. Malloy, ed., *Authoritarianism and Corporatism in Latin America* (Pittsburgh: University of Pittsburgh Press, 1977).

13 Good discussions of state capitalism in the Third World are found in J. P. Perez Sainz, 'Towards a Conceptualization of State Capitalism in the Periphery,' *The Insurgent Sociologist* 9, no. 4 (Spring 1980); Alex Dupuy and Barry Truchil, 'Problems in the Theory of State Capitalism,' *Theory and Society* 8, no. 1 (July 1979); and William L. Canak, 'The Peripheral State Debate: State Capitalism and Bureaucratic Authoritarian Regimes in Latin America,' *Latin American Research Review* 19, no. 1 (1984).

the state apparatus and which takes over the historical role of the domestic capitalist class in the now-advanced capitalist countries. James Petras identifies the bureaucracy of the state capitalist regime as an 'intermediate strata' that, having a world view shaped by a bureaucratic milieu, functions as an independent class with its own political–economic project. It is the only social force, he argues, that lacks direct ties to landed and imperial interests and is capable of directing a bourgeois revolution through the state.[14] This notion has been strongly opposed, however, on the grounds that those in charge of the state lack an independent basis of capital accumulation.[15]

Although some observers see state capitalism as representing the rule of the lower-middle class and presenting the possibility of a transition to socialism, a perhaps more realistic viewpoint maintains that such a state leads to a reinforcement of capitalism.[16] On one hand, the first perspective suggests that state capitalism has authentic possibilities, at least in relation to domestic capital, and that the petty bourgeoisie in charge of the state has various possibilities of action. Although it is argued that there is no economic transformation in such cases, reformist measures

---

14 James Petras, 'State Capitalism and the Third World,' *Development and Change* 8, no. 1 (1977): 3.
15 E. V. K. Fitzgerald, 'On State Accumulation in Latin America,' in E. V. K. Fitzgerald et al., eds., *The State and Economic Development in Latin America* (Cambridge: University Printing House, 1977), p. 66; Michaela Von Freyhold, 'The Post-Colonial State and Its Tanzanian Version,' *Review of African Political Economy*, no. 8 (January–April 1971): 85; Bernardo Sorj, 'Public Enterprise and the Question of the State Bourgeoisie,' in David Booth and Bernard Sorj, eds., *Military Reformism and Social Classes: The Peruvian Experience, 1968–1976* (London: Macmillan, 1983), p. 74.
16 Examples of this former viewpoint include M. Kalecki, 'Observations on Social and Economic Aspects of Intermediate Regime,' in Michel Kalecki, ed., *Essays on Developing Countries* (Hassocks, Eng.: Harvester Press, 1976); Kenneth Jameson, 'An Intermediate Regime in Historical Context: The Case of Guyana,' *Development and Change* 11, no. 1 (January 1980); Thanos Skouras, 'The "Intermediate Regime" and Industrialization,' *Development and Change* 9, no. 4 (October 1978); Berch Berberoglu, 'State Capitalism and National Industrialization in Turkey,' *Development and Change* 11, no. 1 (June 1980). The latter viewpoint often points out that nationalizations may benefit local capitalists while joint ventures reduce risks and help to increase profits. See, for example, E. V. K. Fitzgerald, 'Some Aspects of the Political Economy of the Latin American State,' *Development and Change* 7, no. 2 (April 1976); and Nora Hamilton, 'The State and the National Bourgeoisie in Post-Revolutionary Mexico,' *Latin American Perspectives* 9, no. 4 (Fall 1982).

of such regimes are seen as genuine, reflecting the ambiguities of
the petty bourgeoisie in charge of the state and the genuine
commitment of at least one faction of it to reform. The opposing
view, on the other hand, argues that even in its reformist form,
the Third World state serves to reinforce capitalism, that dependence continues in the form of joint ventures, technological
dependence, and rising foreign debt, and that eventually
measures will have to be taken to contain labors' demands as
these demands begin to have a negative impact on profits.

In fact, many observers claim a growing alliance between the
Third World state and big capital, especially foreign capital. Local
capital, it has been suggested, is now becoming the junior partner
in a symbiosis or triangular relationship with the state, the local
bourgeoisie, and foreign capital.[17] Measures opening the
economy to foreign competition or direct foreign investment may
be harmful to indigenous capital. This alliance with multinational
capital reinforced by military and political linkages in many cases
gives the state even more institutional independence from the
local bourgeoisie. The growing concentration of economic power
in the hands of the Third World state and its seemingly close
relationship with multinational capital has prompted the notion
of 'state monopoly capitalism,' characterized by an increase in
state expenditures that benefits the monopoly bourgeoisie while
the national or indigenous bourgeoisie is replaced.[18] In a number
of cases the state has been able to maneuver for itself a prominent
role in alliance with multinational capital while increasing its
power in relation to local capital. Hence, the Third World state
would appear to be in some ways weaker and in other ways
stronger than its counterpart in the developed capitalist world.

---

17 See for example Peter Evans, 'Multinationals: State-Owned Corporations and
    the Transformation of Imperialism: A Brazilian Case Study,' *Economic Develop-*
    ment and Cultural Change 26, no. 1 (October 1977): 43; Steven Langdon, 'The
    State and Capitalism in Kenya,' *Review of African Political Economy*, no. 8
    (January–April 1977): 95; Thomas Bamat, 'Relative State Autonomy and Capi-
    talism in Brazil and Peru,' *The Insurgent Sociologist* 7, no. 1 (Spring 1977): 22.
18 It has been suggested, however, that the term 'state monopoly capitalism' is
    inappropriate as it implies a qualitatively new phenomenon—signified by the
    fusion of the state and monopoly capital—that is not the case. For a critical
    discussion of the term, see Alex Dupuy and Barry Tuchil, 'Problems in the
    Theory of State Capitalism,' *Theory and Society* 8, no. 1 (July 1979): 16.

Although it may have more autonomy relative to indigenous propertied classes due to their historical weakness and due to the divisions within them, the Third World state is weak since it usually lacks resources sufficient to carry out its legitimization function, and, since at the same time it is subject to manipulation from external sources.

There is general consensus in the literature that the Third World state makes manageable the class struggle through some combination of cooptation and repression depending upon the form of regime.[19] It is rarely seen as the mere instrument of either the propertied classes or foreign capital. It is generally agreed that the Third World state has 'relative autonomy,' from both domestic business groups and international capital, although the extent of that autonomy is an issue of considerable debate. The possibilities created by a reformist, interventionist state whose policies apparently benefit the popular classes and indigenous capital is also a contentious issue. Stronger than the indigenous propertied classes, the Third World state is expected to play some role in mediating both the disagreements within indigenous capital and between indigenous capital and multinational capital. The extent to which it is able to carry out such a role is, however, open to question.

The Third World State and the Problem of Policy Formulation

There is no clear consensus on the nature and role of the Third World state. On one hand, one might argue that the specific conditions and histories of the countries lumped together in such an amorphous category as the 'Third World' defy any sort of theoretical generalization. On the other, contradictions in state action are found not only among Third World countries but

---

19 Fernando Henrique Cardoso's distinction between form of state and form of regime is important here. While the term *state* is used to describe the system of domination—that is, the relationship between the dominant classes and the state—*regime* refers to the manner in which control is exercised by state managers who may or may not be part of the dominant alliance. Fernando Henrique Cardoso, 'On the Characterization of Authoritarian Regimes in Latin America,' in David Collier, ed., *The New Authoritarianism in Latin America* (Princeton, NJ: Princeton University Press, 1979).

within particular countries. Hence, different observers may see
distinct possibilities. State action may appear to reverse itself
from one historical period to the next, causing observers to claim
that a transition to a new phase is occurring. But even within a
very short time span not only may official rhetoric contradict
official policy but specific policies may contradict each other. The
problem is compounded by the thorny question of whether the
results of state policy are those intended by the state. There is, as
a consequence, invariably a heated dispute over the issue of the
'real' objectives of the state. What does one make, for example, of
a situation in which legislation is passed to restrict foreign capital
while the state allows that legislation to be violated in its
implementation, or a situation in which some firms are nationalized while others are heavily subsidized allowing high profits to
the owners? How does one interpret state action that vacillates
between repression of the labor movement and consent to its
demands?

In general such phenomena are looked at in two ways. It is
often argued that the state's real objective is to preserve capitalism and work in the long-term interests of the capitalist class,
usually defined as the most powerful, indigenous private-sector
interests and their foreign allies. In this case any measures taken
to benefit labor are tactics to ensure the existing order. Or it is
argued instead that the real objective of those in charge of the
state (a reformist faction of the state bourgeoisie) is to support
measures that stimulate national development and benefit the
popular classes. In this latter case, measures benefiting foreign
and domestic business stem from the pressure exerted from
powerful domestic and foreign business interests the ruling
group has failed to destroy. While it is not realistic to view the
Third World state as having as its primary objective the expansion of the political and economic power of the popular classes, it
is equally erroneous to assume that whatever action the state
takes is in the long-term interests of capitalism. Both of these
views assume a logic and coherence of the state that is not the
case.

The apparent relative autonony that supposedly characterizes
the Third World state must not be allowed to obscure the fact that
the state, as one aspect of the social relations of capital, is—in the

words of John Holloway and Sol Piciotto—'stamped throughout in all its institutions, procedures and ideology with the contradictions of capital.'[20] The state is a focus of class conflict. Through it the conflicts between class and fractions of the dominant class are incorporated and transformed. Because the overriding interest of state managers is the perpetuation of the existing political order, there is an ongoing effort to institutionalize (make manageable) the contradictions of the social order. This conceptualization assumes that the state is at once cohesive and fragmented. The factor of state cohesion is the unifying motivation of state managers to preserve the existing political order. This means that political criteria will predominate over all other considerations. At the same time, the state becomes fragmented insofar as it becomes the focus of class and intraclass struggles. Hence, various departments, institutions, and agencies of the state reflect these struggles, ideally in a way that does not disrupt the political order. State institutions vary in their susceptibility to societal contradictions. Some more than others are able to reflect bureaucratic interests, because they are more insulated from societal conflicts.

As class struggle intensifies it is to be expected that contradictions within the state will also intensify. Hence, different agencies of the state may come to 'represent' opposing interests as certain factions of domestic or international capital find their access to the state at different points, and as bureaucrats at these points of access internalize the policy orientations of specific outside interests. Close links have been observed for example between parastates in Third World countries and multinational capital.[21] Close links and an affinity of views have also been found between officials of central banks and departments of commerce and the private sector, while planning agencies tend to be more reformist in their orientation.[22]

The nature and direction of state expansion (or its retraction)

---

20 John Holloway and Sol Piciotto, 'Capital, Crisis and the State,' in *Capital and Class*, no. 2 (Summer 1977): 76.

21 Timothy M. Shaw, 'Zambia: Dependence and Underdevelopment,' *Canadian Journal of African Studies* 10, no. 1 (1976): 17.

22 Bernardo Sorj, 'Public Enterprises and the Question of the State Bourgeoisie,' in David Booth and Bernard Sorj, *Military Reformism and Social Classes*, p. 88.

reflect a response to social issues and the state's goal of maintaining the political order. The need to reconcile contradictory pressures from business and the popular classes may, for example, propel the state into more intervention despite insufficient resources. This increasing interventionism is likely to create new unforeseen tensions with the private sector while producing new expectations on the part of the popular classes. These tensions are likely to adversely affect private-sector investment decisions. Political necessity demands that these tensions and expectations be further managed by the state in a manner conducive to the maintenance of the political order. Decisions made with this objective in mind may be politically rational in the short term but economically counterproductive in the medium and long term.

If we assume that the contradictions of capitalism are reproduced within the state, then it is questionable whether the state can ever act in the interests of capital as a whole. Conflicts within society and the manner in which these conflicts are reconciled would inevitably inhibit the state from designing and implementing coherent and consistent economic policies.

This is not to deny the important impact that state interests may have on policy. Indeed, the precise manner in which the conflicts between the propertied classes and the masses—and between factions of the propertied classes—are filtered and transformed within the state must be understood within the context of the interests and motivations of state managers. We cannot, however, consider state managers a separate class. Lacking their own independent basis of capital accumulation, this group may be conceived of as a 'social category,' acknowledging its predominance in certain economic sectors and a limited degree of overall cohesiveness.[23]

While the framework of policy is set by the operation of capitalism and by the class context in which state managers are performing, the choice of specific policies resides in the hands of state managers as they respond to societal conflicts. It is the interaction between these societal conflicts and political–bureaucratic interests that, we argue, explains state policy. State

---

23 Nicos Poulantzas, *Political Power and Social Class* (London: Sheed and Ward, 1973), p. 4.

policy, moreover, may just as easily exacerbate class conflict and deepen economic crisis as alleviate political and economic crisis.

The State and Policymaking in Mexico: The Debate over State Autonomy

The Mexican state has played a central role in the evolution of Mexican capitalism. The inheritors of the Mexican Revolution, the professional and landed middle classes who came to man the state apparatus, presided over the period of state-led economic growth known as the 'Mexican miracle.' During this period— between 1940 and 1965 when growth rates averaged 6 per cent— the Mexican state accomplished the unlikely task of maintaining popular legitimacy in the face of rising inequalities, both in relative and absolute terms.[24] With the exception of the 1968 student massacre at Tlatelolco, violent repression on any sizeable scale has not been necessary. In this one-party-dominant system, legitimacy has been fostered and unrest controlled by the more subtle means of a revolutionary mythology, cooptation, selected reforms, and socialization; state violence has been only a last resort. The apparent success of the Mexican state in fostering dependent capitalist development while containing political unrest has been the focus of a great deal of scholarly writing.[25]

Few observers of recent political events in Mexico have characterized the Mexican state as a neutral arbiter of conflicting social classes.[26] Most argue that the state's autonomy from the domestic

---

24 Indeed Roger Hansen suggests that 'the degree of inequality in the distribution of Mexican income exceeds that of most of the world's developing countries': *The Politics of Mexican Development* (Baltimore: Johns Hopkins University Press, 1980), p. 83. On the increasing inequality brought about by Mexico's post-1940 development model, see Ifigenia M. de Navarrete, 'Income Distribution in Mexico,' in Enrique Pérez López et al., eds., *Mexico's Recent Economic Growth* (Austin: University of Texas Press, 1965).

25 See references cited in footnote 34.

26 Some of the best-known earlier work that characterizes the Mexican state as a neutral arbiter includes Charles C. Cumberland, *Mexico: The Struggle for Modernity* (New York: Oxford University Press, 1968); L. Vincent Padgett, *The Mexican Political System* (Boston: Houghton Mifflin, 1966); Robert E. Scott, *Mexican Government in Transition* (Urbana: University of Illinois Press, 1964). Padgett's second, 1976 edition, however, notes the preponderant influence of urban professional and business groups. Although the notion of the Mexican

and foreign business sectors is only relative. The form of regime, it is generally agreed, is authoritarian, especially as it pertains to the popular classes.[27] The PRI (the Institutional Revolutionary Party) is not seen as a mechanism that facilitates the participation of the popular classes in politics but rather as a mechanism of political control. As some have pointed out, the Mexican political system is characterized by an absence of autonomous publics ('limited pluralism') and by low political participation. Mexico has a heterogeneous, pragmatic, and nonideological elite that maintains political control through an elaborate system of patron clientelism. Policy—unfettered by the need to consult important groups beforehand—tends to be pragmatic and geared toward the strengthening of the political elite through the dispensing of tangible rewards. Public participation in the policymaking process is heavily discouraged. Indeed, the Mexican state reacts to organized groups pressing for policy change 'as if it were dealing with enemy nations.'[28] Far from seeing any discernible move toward democracy, it has been suggested that the system is becoming more authoritarian, especially prior to the political reform of 1977.[29]

state as neutral arbiter has been largely rejected, it can still be found. See for example Martin C. Needler, *Mexican Politics: The Containment of Conflict* (New York: Praeger, 1982).

27 On the application of Juan Linz's conceptualization of authoritarian regimes to Mexico, see especially Susan Kaufman Purcell, 'Decision Making in an Authoritarian Regime: Theoretical Implications of a Mexican Case Study,' *World Politics* 26, no. 1 (October 1973). Also see Juan J. Linz, 'An Authoritarian Regime: Spain,' in Erik Allardt and Stein Rokkan, eds., *Mass Politics* (New York: Free Press, 1970).

28 Evelyn Stevens, *Protest and Response in Mexico* (Cambridge, MA: MIT Press, 1974), p. 259.

29 See for example Evelyn Stevens, *Protest and Response in Mexico*, p. 20; José Luis Reyna, 'Control politico: estabilidad y desarrollo en México,' *Cuadernos del CES*, núm. 3, p. 27. There has also been some attempt to explain why Mexican authoritarianism has been more benign than that which occurred in the Southern cone during the 1970s. One of the more interesting explanations suggests that because authoritarian corporate controls were already in place in Mexico when industrialization began, the new phase that was to entail the transition to import substitution in intermediate and capital goods could be embarked upon smoothly with the mechanisms already in place to contain political unrest, making violent repression less necessary. Robert R. Kaufman, 'Mexico and Latin American Authoritarianism,' in José Luis Reyna and Richard J. Weinert, eds., *Authoritarianism in Mexico* (Philadelphia: Institute for the Study of Human Issues, 1977).

Although there is general agreement that the Mexican state is authoritarian and that the state's autonomy from the private sector is not absolute, there is considerable dispute over the question of the extent of this relative autonomy. Here we may distinguish three fairly distinct outlooks, each representing different points on a continuum regarding the question of capital's influence—foreign and indigenous—over the policymaking process and the coalescence of political and business elites.

The first perspective stresses the interlocks between Mexico's political and economic elites. It assumes a tight coherence between these elite groups and argues that policy stems from the coincidence of interests that holds these elite groups together. This power elite—referred to as the 'revolutionary family' in its earliest formulations, or the 'oligarchy'—experiences disagreements among its various factions that are said to be of minor or secondary importance.[30] In the most recent studies the situation has been characterized as one of domination by state monopoly capitalism, a close alliance between the state, foreign capital, and big indigenous-business interests. Policy, then—according to this viewpoint—reflects more and more the interests of this power elite in which monopoly capital, both domestic and foreign, is dominant. Whatever relative autonomy the state may have had to act in the interests of the popular classes or to constrain monopoly interests has virtually disappeared.[31] Nor is it possible any longer to attribute an important role to state interests in the formulation of policy. Despite the fact that the Mexican state has a large role in development, the triple alliance

---

30 Examples of this position include Frank Brandenburg, *The Making of Modern Mexico* (Englewood Cliffs, NJ: Prentice-Hall, 1964); Alonso Aquilar M. and Fernando Carmona, *México: Riqueza y miseria* (México, D.F.: Editorial Nuestro Tiempo, S.A., 1972); James D. Cockcroft, *Mexico: Class Formation, Capital Accumulation and the State* (New York: Monthly Review Press, 1983); Ramiro Reyes Esparza et al., *La burguesía mexicana*, 3d ed. (México, D.F.: Editorial Nuestro Tiempo, S.A., 1978).

31 Recent examples of this viewpoint include, Steven E. Sanderson, *Agrarian Populism and the Mexican State* (Berkeley: University of California Press, 1981), pp. 201–202; Juan M. Martínez Nova, *Conflicto estado empresarios* (México, D.F.: Editorial Nueva Imagen, 1984), pp. 56–57; Julio La Bastida Martín del Campo, 'Los grupos dominantes frente las alternativas de cambio,' in Jorge Martínez Ríos et al., eds., *El perfil de México en 1980*, 7th ed., vol. 3 (México, D.F.: Siglo XXI Editores, S.A., 1980), p. 126.

between the state, foreign capital, and powerful indigenous business interests has meant, in the words of one Mexico specialist, that 'the orientation of this development has been largely determined by foreign and national capital.'[32] Indeed, many maintain that domestic capital has by now become the junior partner.[33] The evidence for the predominance of the power elite is found not in the analysis of policy formulation but in the concrete outcome of policy itself. Because economic policy in Mexico over the last forty years has, on the whole, benefited powerful business interests, it is assumed that these business interests have manipulated state policy in their interests.

The second viewpoint is less comfortable with the notion of a cohesive ruling oligarchy and places Mexican business interests and their foreign allies in the position of the most powerful social group, though not in charge of the state.[34] This perspective allows for the existence of a distinct political–bureaucratic elite and state interest, but argues that in most cases business interests will prevail in public policy. This perspective emphasizes the controls the private sector exercises over the state and downplays the sanctions the state has at its disposal to modify the behavior of private capital. The private sector, it is pointed out, can veto policies with which it disagrees most effectively by sending capital out of the country, but it can also have an effect through its

32 Nora Hamilton, *The Limits of State Autonomy: Post-Revolutionary Mexico* (Princeton, NJ: Princeton University Press, 1982), p. 32.
33 Ignacio Hernández Gutiérrez, 'La burguesía commercial nativa y el capital extranjero' in Romero Reyes Esparza et al., eds., *La burguesía mexicana* (México, D.F.: Editorial Nuestro Tiempo, 1978), p. 196; Jorge Carrión, 'La inversión extranjera y el desarrollo del imperialismo,' in Alonso Aguilar M. et al., *Política mexicana sobre inversiones extranjeras* (México, D.F.: UNAM, 1977), p. 28 ff.; Julio La Bastida Martín del Campo, 'Los grupos dominantes frente a las alternativas de cambio,' p. 132. This point has been disputed by de la Peña, who argues that in state monopoly capitalism 'the national bourgeoisie does not disappear, but rather is strengthened and invigorated': 'Proletarian Power and State Monopoly Capitalism in Mexico,' *Latin American Perspectives* 9, no. 1 (Winter 1982): 29.
34 See for example Roger D. Hansen, *The Politics of Mexican Development* (Baltimore: Johns Hopkins University Press, 1980); Daniel Levy and Gabriel Szekély, *Mexico: Paradoxes of Stability and Change* (Boulder, CO: Westview Press, 1983); Judith Adler Hellman, *Mexico in Crisis*, 2d ed. (New York: Holmes and Meier, 1983); E. V. K. Fitzgerald, 'The State and Capital Accumulation in Mexico,' *Journal of Latin American Studies* 10, no. 2 (November 1978); González Casanova, *Democracy in Mexico* (New York: Oxford University Press, 1970).

[15]

control over the mass means of communication and through opportunities for personal influence.[35] This second perspective tends to emphasize the mechanisms by which the popular sectors are controlled: the manipulation of revolutionary symbols and mythology, selective political and economic reforms, the cooptation of dissidents and potential dissidents through captured labor organizations, and the frequent circulation of bureaucratic and political jobs. Like the power-elite perspective, this viewpoint looks at policy output. Reforms in the interest of the popular sector are not impossible, but when they occur they will be selective, to be regarded as mechanisms in the cooptation process. Typically, the state handles opposition initially through attempted cooptation, followed by repression if cooptation fails, and finally by a delayed response to the grievances that fueled the mobilization in the first place.

This viewpoint maintains that the autonomy of the state has been limited, that the state has acted fairly consistently in the interests of capital, especially the most powerful capitalist groups, while measures in the interests of the popular classes have been only those necessary to buy off discontent and maintain the political order by shoring up the state's legitimacy.[36] Although the state may be capable of acting against the specific interests of some capitalists, it is not capable of controlling the private sector in the long term. The state's small margin of relative autonomy allows it to institute preemptive reforms and to act against specific capitalist interests thereby ensuring political stability, preserving the capitalist system, and acting in the long-term interests of all capitalists.

The final viewpoint acknowledges the political importance of the private sector but argues that its control over state action is less than commonly assumed. Much of the work supporting this

---

35 On the private sector's manipulation of the mass media to influence public opinion, see Angela M. Delli Santo, 'The Private Sector, Business Organizations and International Influence,' in Richard R. Fagen, ed., *Capitalism and the State in U.S.–Latin American Relations* (Stanford, CA: Stanford University Press, 1981).

36 On the efficacy of preemptive reforms during the Echeverría and López Portillo years, see Kenneth M. Coleman and Charles L. Davis, 'Preemptive Reform and the Mexican Working Class,' *Latin American Research Review* 18, no. 1 (1983).

viewpoint analyzes the formulation of specific policies.[37] This perspective emphasizes the control the state has over the private sector, points out that the state usually takes the initiative in policy formulation, and argues that state maneuverability in the policy realm is not only influenced by business interests but is also constrained by popular demands. According to this viewpoint, one can speak of an identifiable state interest that pursues policies which—although they may have benefited the private sector—spring from different concerns and have been undertaken without pressure from the business community. The assumption here is that the state has an identifiable will, distinguishable from that of the private sector and that it has the ability to enforce that will against the wishes of the private sector. This viewpoint has been reinforced by recent work demonstrating the distinct social and educational backgrounds of political and business leaders.[38]

Proponents of this last viewpoint consider state controls over the private sector to be effective. This control springs not just from the state's general control over the economy but also from its control over credits, tariffs, import permits, licenses, tax

---

37 Most notable examples of this perspective include the works of Susan Kaufman Purcell, among them *The Mexican Profit Sharing Decision* (Berkeley: University of California Press, 1975); Raymond Vernon, *The Dilemma of Mexico's Development* (Cambridge, MA: Harvard University Press, 1963); Richard S. Weinert, 'The State and Foreign Capital,' in José Luis Reyna and Richard S. Weinert, eds., *Authoritarianism in Mexico*; Miguel Basáñez, *La lucha por la hegemonía en México, 1968–1980*, 2d ed. (Mexico, D.F.: Siglo XXI, 1982); Américo Saldívar, *Ideología y política del estado mexicano, 1970–1976* (Mexico, D.F.: Siglo XXI, 1980); Douglas Bennett, Morris Blackman, and Kenneth Sharpe, 'Mexico and Multinational Corporations: An Explanation of State Action,' in Joseph Greenwald, ed., *Latin America and World Economy: A Changing International Order*) Newbury Park, CA: Sage Publications, 1978); Douglas C. Bennett and Kenneth E. Sharpe, 'Agenda Setting and Bargaining Power: The Mexican State Versus the Transnational Automobile Corporations,' in *World Politics* XXXII, no. 1 (October 1979); Martin Harry Greenberg, *Bureaucracy and Development: A Mexican Case Study* (Lexington, MA: D. C. Heath, 1970); Merilee S. Grindle, *Bureaucrats, Politicians and Peasants in Mexico* (Berkeley: University of California Press, 1977); Rose J. Spalding, 'Welfare Policy Making: Theoretical Implications of a Mexican Case Study,' *Comparative Politics* 12, no. 2 (July 12, 1980).

38 Roderic A. Camp, *Mexico's Leaders* (Tucson: University of Arizona Press, 1980); and Peter Smith, *Labyrinths of Power* (Princeton, NJ: Princeton University Press, 1979).

exemptions, and public facilities. Furthermore, the very extensiveness of the state's involvement in the economy, it is argued, gives the state considerable leverage over the private sector. The state's decisions about how or where to invest, given the importance of state investment, may be critical for potential or existing investments by the private sector. Furthermore, splits within the bourgeoisie are said to further strengthen the state in the face of the private sector. The Mexican state, it is argued, is unusual in the pervasiveness and discriminatory application of its regulatory powers. Indeed, it has been suggested that 'the private sector operates in a milieu in which the public sector is in a position to make or break any private firm.'[39]

Although separated organically and structurally from the bourgeoisie, state managers are considered part of the dominant class if not its predominant faction. The group in charge of the state is seen as engaged in a political struggle for dominance with the forces of the private sector. By the mid-1970s this struggle had become so tense that it has been characterized as one of a 'political tie' as the most powerful entrepreneurial forces gain momentum.[40] According to Peter Smith, entrepreneurs and politicians are 'Locked in a struggle for supremacy' and 'interact within an atmosphere of uncertainty, distrust, suspicion and even disdain.'[41] Observers point to the escalating level of tension between the private sector and the state during the regime of President Luis Echeverría (1970–1976) as evidence of the intensity of this struggle.

Despite the fact that state policy has benefited the private sector, numerous studies have pointed out that many policies have not been initiated by the private sector. It would appear that the private sector does not directly shape state policy. Furthermore, the government has pursued policies contrary to the wishes and interests of capitalists, which they have been induced by various means to accept.[42] It is also pointed out that constraints

---

39 Raymond Vernon, *The Dilemma of Mexico's Development*, p. 26.
40 Américo Saldívar, *Ideología y política del estado mexicano, 1970–1976*, p. 173.
41 Peter H. Smith, *Labyrinths of Power*, p. 211.
42 See for example Susan Kaufman Purcell, *The Mexican Profit-Sharing Decision*; and 'Business–Government Relations in Mexico: The Case of the Sugar Industry,' *Comparative Politics*, 13, no. 2 (January 1981).

are placed upon policymakers by the popular classes. While acknowledging that reforms benefiting the popular classes answer to the state's interest in warding off discontent, this viewpoint nevertheless argues the importance of anticipated popular response in the formulation of such policies as price controls on basic commodities. There may also be the recognition of a reformist faction among state managers which shares a genuine commitment to the redistributive and nationalist goals of the Mexican Revolution.[43] Indeed, popular support may be important in effectively bargaining with the dominant economic classes. In its emphasis on the economic power of the state, on the importance of distinctive state interests in the formulation of policy, and on the possibility of genuine reformist policies benefiting the popular classes, this perspective approximates the reformist state-capitalist notion discussed earlier.

Although in general the economic model pursued by the Mexican state has benefited the capitalist class (including foreign capital), specific policies have not always sprung from pressure emanating from the private sector and have, not infrequently, been contrary to its wishes and/or interests. It is necessary to reexamine the notion of relative autonomy and to explain the contradictory thrusts of state policy within a framework that recognizes the state as imbedded in the economic and social order, as a focus of class and intraclass struggle, but also as an institution through which societal interests may be transformed or filtered by political–bureaucratic interests. The premise that the contradictions of capitalism are reproduced within the state and interact with political–bureaucratic interests renders the notion of relative autonomy highly problematic and allows us to explain the often inconsistent nature of policy.

Mexico, 1976–1982: The Argument of the Book

This book is a study of economic policymaking in Mexico focusing upon the *sexenio* (the six-year term) of López Portillo—the era

---

43 See for example Carlos Tello, *La política económica en México, 1970–1976* (México, D.F.: Siglo XXI, 1980), p. 62.

of the petroleum boom, the 1982 economic crisis, and the eventual bank nationalization. This was an administration marked by sharp contradictions in policy: it began by restoring the confidence of the private sector through a model of petroleum-based capital-intensive growth, fiscal incentives, subsidies, and tax writeoffs; yet it ended its days by profoundly alienating that sector through its nationalization of the private banks, long a target of leftist groups and a symbol of privileged and oligarchical economic domination. The administration that had been for years criticized by its leftist opponents for its single-minded preoccupation with selling off Mexican resources (petroleum and gas) and for its treatment of peasants, reached its finale in popular adulation as the left hailed the return of a new 'Cárdenismo.'

Faced with economic crisis in 1976 and again in 1982, the maneuverability of the state became increasingly circumscribed. This book argues that to defend the political order in the short term the state took actions that were counterproductive to the smooth functioning of Mexico's capitalism. The concept of 'relative autonomy' has limited usefulness, insofar as it is meant to connote the ability of the state to act cohesively in the long-term interests of peripheral capitalism and the capitalist class. It is argued that the Mexican state is a fragmented and therefore weak state, despite the fact that it is capable of taking the initiative in policy and despite the presence of a very large state sector and socially distinct political and bureaucratic elite. Permeated by the contradictions of peripheral capitalism and preoccupied with the need to satisfy private sector and bureaucratic clienteles while perpetuating the political order, the Mexican state proved incapable of pursuing a coherent economic program between 1976 and 1982.

But although state actions, or lack of them, were instrumental in deepening Mexico's growing economic crisis, both the crises of the late 1960s and of 1982 had their historical roots in Mexico's state-led industrialization process. The economic strategy pursued during the sexenio of President López Portillo was an attempt to confront the political and economic dilemma of the late 1960s, which President Echeverría's strategy had failed to solve. And it was an attempt that was defined by the increasingly narrow parameters of Mexico's peripheral capitalism. The following chapters trace the historical roots and evolution of that strategy. Therein we argue that the goals and interests of state managers have interacted with the growing contradictions of peripheral capitalism and with international events, producing policies that have deepened Mexico's economic crisis and exacerbated social conflicts.

2
Historical Roots of the 1982 Crisis

Introduction

While the historical roots of Mexico's 1982 economic crisis are to be found in the state's post-1940 economic model, the success with which the state implemented that model had its origins in the political arrangements worked out as a result of the 1910–1917 Mexican Revolution. The establishment of an authoritarian corporatist state—a centralized state that has been highly successful at incorporating the popular sectors within the party–state apparatus—assured the social peace that made a program of rapid modernization possible. The Constitution of 1917 and the subsequent evolution of the state apparatus ensured the instruments necessary for an activist role in the economy.

Political Roots: The Origins of the Authoritarian Corporatist State

The emergence of the modern Mexican state, a state capable of absorbing political unrest through a combination of revolutionary mythology and a web of patron clientelism and corporatist institutional arrangements, was by no means a smooth one. It emerged only with the costly trauma of the Mexican Revolution. Even then, it showed continuities with the prerevolutionary period.

It was under the auspices of the *Porfiriato* (the regime of Porfirio Díaz, 1876–1911) that Mexico was fully integrated into the international division of labor as a mineral-export enclave, and it was

[23]

under the guidance of the Porfiriato's *científicos*, high-ranking administrators who believed national problems could be solved by scientific solutions, that Mexico embarked upon a program of modernization and incipient industrialization. Although the state played an important role in this early industrialization process, its role was clearly one of providing infrastructure and incentives for private investment. The prerevolutionary Mexican state was a liberal state, with the paramountcy of property rights taking precedence over all other social values. In its effort to stimulate industrialization, the railway system was rapidly expanded, ports were improved, and internal tariffs inhibiting local trade were abolished. The científico belief in things foreign and the denigration of anything indigenous, produced vigorous efforts to attract foreign investment, especially into such areas as mining and petroleum.

The results based on economic indicators were encouraging: silver production quadrupled, and Mexico became the world's second-largest copper producer. Industrialization began in Monterrey and Nuevo León, with the volume of manufactured goods doubling during the period.[1] The government's philosophy of 'order and progress' and a surplus in the treasury firmly established Mexico's credit rating. However, there were clearly negative aspects to the modernization program. Legislation designed to attract railway companies and the systematic enforcement of legislation to create private property from Indian lands had divested the peasantry of their holdings. By 1910 less than 1 percent of families owned or controlled 85 percent of the land.[2] Agriculture, because of the incapacity of the *latifundia* (large land holdings) to carry out technological changes or improve productivity, could not keep up with population growth. The most important sectors of the economy were in foreign hands: mining, transportation, sugar, coffee plantations, and cattle ranches—along with banking—were all dominated by foreign ownership. The trappings of modernization had not touched the vast majority of the population. It has been estimated

1 Robert Ryal Miller, *Mexico: A History* (Norman: University of Oklahoma Press, 1985), p. 449.
2 Charles Cumberland, *Mexican Revolution: Genesis under Madero* (Austin: University of Texas Press, 1952), p. 22.

that in 1910 real wages of the Mexican peon were one-quarter of what they had been in 1800.[3] Moreover, politically the system was rigid, making no room for even the participation of the new professional and middle-class groups that had arisen with the modernization program. The northern bourgeoisie, excluded from the benefits of the Porfiriato, was particularly frustrated. Porfirio Díaz had ruled through press censorship, manipulated elections, cooptation, and often outright repression.[4] Since the Mexican economy was closely integrated with the American, the Wall Street crisis of 1907 further deepened the economic misery of the masses and the political frustration of the new middle-class groups and propelled the overthrow of a regime that had come to be identified almost entirely with foreign capital interests.

But while the Mexican Revolution was to produce some fundamental changes in the power structure—bringing to power middle-class professional and bourgeois groups excluded from political power during the Porfiriato and incorporating in a subordinate way workers and peasants—significant continuities remained. Mexico was an enclave economy with important economic sectors still in the hands of foreigners. Moreover some of the most powerful indigenous groups, such as the industrialists of Monterrey (the 'Monterrey group'), survived the revolution.

Although the interests of workers and peasants would be largely ignored until the rebirth of the Mexican Revolution under President Lázaro Cárdenas (1934–1940), their rights were acknowledged in a symbolic sense. The strength of an incipient labor movement and the continued violence springing from land hunger had forced the recognition of popular grievances. Hence, the Constitution of 1917 reflected the tension between social interest and liberal values which has been a constant characteristic of Mexican public policy.[5] The hardships wrought upon the

---

3 Henry Bamford Parkes, *A History of Mexico* (London: Eyre and Spottiswoode, 1960), p. 96.

4 For an in-depth examination of one of the most important mainstays of the Porfiriato, the feared rural police force known as the *rurales* and their relationship to the process of economic modernization, see Paul J. Vanderwood, *Disorder and Progress* (Lincoln: University of Nebraska Press, 1981).

5 On the intellectual antecedents of this ideological division, see James Cockcroft, *Intellectual Precursors of the Mexican Revolution* (Austin: University of Texas Press, 1968).

masses by the liberalism of the Porfiriato gave rise to the notion of a broader social interest. Opposing moderate-liberal (chiefly Carranza's followers) and radical factions (a group with nominal allegiance to Obregón led by General Francisco Múgica) clashed over such issues as worker rights, social legislation, property rights, and state ownership of the subsoil. While moderates invoked a more or less orthodox liberal ideology, radicals advocated a strong state that would generate social reforms.[6]

It was at the behest of the radicals led by General Francisco Múgica that Articles 27 and 123 of the 1917 Constitution were adopted. Article 27 denied the absolute right of private property, declaring it subordinate to public welfare, and declared the nation to be the owner of all lands and waters. Article 123, perhaps the most advanced labor code of its day, provided for the protection of wage earners. Hence, the Constitution established the central responsibility of the state for economic development and social reforms. It also established the presidency as predominant over all other branches of government.

Institutionalization of the Authoritarian Corporatist State

It was with the presidency of Alvaro Obregón (1920–1924) that the long process of institutionalization began; that is, the evolution of an accepted process for the orderly transfer of power and for the more or less orderly management of dissent or potential dissent. It was also during the Obregón years—and especially during the years of President Plutarco Elías Calles (1924–1934)—that the basic economic instruments of the Mexican state were established.

From the establishment of the earliest postrevolutionary governments, the political elite saw the importance of maintaining the support of labor and peasants and of tightening control over them. From the beginning the government's strategy appears to have been to prevent unified independent organizations of workers and peasants from emerging by coopting lead-

---

6 James A. Wilkie, *The Mexican Revolution: Federal Expenditures and Social Change Since 1910* (Berkeley: University of California Press, 1967), p. 51.

ers and setting up separate organizations. The dominant labor organization of the 1920s, the CROM (Mexican Regional Workers' Confederation), collaborated closely with the Obregón and Calles administrations. Indeed, during the Calles years the head of CROM, Luis Morones, served as secretary of labor. With full government support, the CROM attempted to destroy the independent labor movement.[7] But it was with the establishment of the PNR (the National Revolutionary Party) in 1929 that the institutional basis of control was definitively established. Created by Calles so that he could maintain political control through his three puppet presidents between 1928 and 1934, it institutionalized previous informal relationships that Obregón had utilized to maintain control. Each of the state political machines (which before had been military) was incorporated into the PNR in return for a share in national patronage and policy making.[8] Patronage, then as now, was the glue that kept the political system together. Those who were loyal had their regions provided with irrigation works, roads, schools, and agricultural credit. The PNR became the political instrument through which all political positions were filled with Calles supporters and the means by which he controlled the next three presidents. By centralizing political control, the party provided the basis for the consolidation of the power of the new political class—those middle-class groups that had risen to power as a result of the revolution.

From the 1920s and particularly during the Calles administration and 'El Maximato' (the three puppet regimes following Calles, 1928–1934), important institutional changes would facilitate the state's ability to lead economic growth. The basis of the Mexican financial system was established. Although Obregón had begun the reconstruction of the banking system destroyed by the revolution, it was not until 1925 that the Bank of Mexico was established as the manager of the nation's gold standard and as the sole bank of issue. But it was only with the Great Depression

7 The CROM broke with the government due to the assassination of Obregón in 1928. The organization disintegrated in the early 1930s with the loss of government support.
8 Howard W. Cline, *The United States and Mexico* (Cambridge, MA: Harvard University Press, 1961), p. 199.

that the Bank was given any real power.[9] According to the 1932 legislation, all commercial banks and important related institutions were now required to become associates of the Banco de México, meaning that they had to purchase small amounts of stock in the Bank and hold a reserve.[10] During the 1930s as well, a number of other important financial institutions were established, the most significant of which was Nacional Financiera (Nafinsa). Established originally in 1933 to sell rural real estate, it would become in later years the principal industrial development arm of the government.

Social reform, on the other hand, had progressed slowly during the 1920s and had practically ground to a halt during the latter years of the corrupt Maximato. Although Obregón had built highways and schools, he had opposed any large-scale redistribution of land. The Calles administration and the three administrations under his dominance also became increasingly conservative as Calles surrounded himself with aging wealthy revolutionaries. Labor was vigorously repressed and agrarian reform virtually abandoned. But the Great Depression, producing a drastic decline in exports and imports and in gross domestic product (GDP), resulted in increasing social unrest and mounting pressure for reform. In 1932 exports were one-third of their 1929 level. Between 1929 and 1932 GDP declined 6.3 percent annually.[11] The economic downturn gave rise to more radical solutions. Even before President Cárdenas came to power in 1934, a younger generation of revolutionaries, many attracted by the Russian experiment, were gaining strength within the party organization. By 1933, as a result of the growing strength of this group, agrarian reform was again on the agenda.[12] Recognizing

9 Initially, private-sector banks were neither required to join the Central Bank nor to submit to its regulations. On this see David H. Shelton, 'The Banking System: Money and the Goal of Growth,' in Raymond Vernon, ed., *Public Policy and Private Enterprise in Mexico* (Cambridge: Cambridge University Press, 1964).

10 Ibid., p. 139.

11 Leopoldo Solís, *La realidad económica mexicana: Retrovisión y perspectivas*, rev. ed. (México, D.F.: Siglo XXI, 1981).

12 Even before Cárdenas took power some important reforms had been instituted. An agrarian code was enacted which transferred the responsibility for the distribution of land from the states to the federal authority, allowing for swifter, more efficient reform. Agricultural banks were reorganized to facili-

the growing strength of the PNR's left wing, Calles decided to choose a successor who would be acceptable to the younger, more radical generation. That choice was Lázaro Cárdenas.

Many studies dealing with the Cárdenas sexenio (1934–1940) have characterized the Mexican state during this period as Bonapartist, as one wherein the weakness of the bourgeoisie and the monetary strength of organized labor and peasants made possible policies in the interests of the popular classes.[13] Indeed, the Cárdenas administration is perhaps best remembered for the extensive reforms carried out to the benefit of the rural popular sector. During Cárdenas' term in office a little over 44 million acres was given out to the peasantry. This administration distributed more land than any other, before or since. Cárdenas spent twice as much on rural education than had any previous president. Credit was increased to the rural sector, and spending on social welfare reached the highest point in Mexican history. Spending on economic—especially agrarian—development reached the highest point since the revolution.[14] Cárdenas placed special emphasis on ejidal holdings in agriculture. The *ejido* is a cooperative form of organization designed to combine economies of scale with traditional communal practices. This type of agricultural organization—encouraged through Cárdenas' land redistribution program, credit, and technical assistance—was expected to produce both domestic and export crops. By 1940

---

tate loans to peasants, and reforms in the area of education raised wages and extended federal authority. Henry Bamford Parkes, *A History of Mexico*, pp. 337–338.

13 Nora Hamilton, *The Limits of State Autonomy: Post-Revolutionary Mexico* (Princeton, NJ: Princeton University Press, 1982), pp. 25, 63; James D. Cockcroft, *Mexico: Class Formation, Capital Accumulation and the State* (New York: Monthly Review Press, 1983), p. 127; Steven E. Sanderson, *Agrarian Reform and the Mexican State* (Berkeley: University of California Press, 1981), p. 196. Manuel Aquilar Mora, *El Bonapartismo mexicano*, vol. 1, 2d ed. (México, D.F.: Juan Pablos Editor, 1984), p. 35.

14 James A. Wilkie, *The Mexican Revolution: Federal Expenditures and Social Change Since 1910*, pp. 136, 157, 159. For a description of how Cárdenas' program improved the daily lives of the rural poor, see Anita Brenner and George R. Leighton, *The Wind that Swept Mexico: The History of the Mexican Revolution, 1910–1942* (Austin: University of Texas Press, 1971), pp. 90–98. On Cárdenas' agrarian reform program see also Nathaniel and Sylvia Weyl, *The Reconquest of Mexico: The Years of Lázaro Cárdenas* (London: Oxford University Press, 1939).

ejido holdings produced 51 percent of the value of farm products.[15]

Cárdenas' agrarian reform program served a number of functions and had important long-term implications for the political system. In destroying the economic basis of the big landlords, the reform strengthened the political power of the new group in charge of the state. The land redistribution program and other social welfare measures did much to increase the popularity of the regime, firmly establishing the official party as the party of the revolution—of the workers and the peasants.

Cárdenas was careful to take measures to consolidate the support he had won. He encouraged the establishment of peasant unions and formed popular militias of workers and peasants, distributing arms to many of the peasant forces. He sponsored the formation of the CNC (National Confederation of Peasants) by means of which he sought to break the power of the landlords. He also gave government backing to the CTM (Confederation of Mexican Workers), an organization representing industrial workers led by Vicente Lombardo Toledano. To wrest control from the Callistas and to consolidate his popular base he reorganized the official party. In 1938 the PNR was reconstituted as the PRM (the Party of the Mexican Revolution). This Party, which was now organized on a sectoral basis rather than on a regional one, was the precursor of the modern-day PRI. The new Party consisted of four sectors: the military, labor, agrarian, and popular sectors. The incorporation of the CTM and the CNC within the PRI was an important change in that it facilitated future centralized control over workers and peasants.[16] Now, with sectoral leadership controlled by the president and offices alloted by sector, political control was centralized in the office of the president. Although Cárdenas may have envisioned that the four sectors would democratically select candidates and that the national sectoral organizations would select the presidential candidate, the system developed in a highly authoritarian fashion in

---

15 Cynthia Hewitt de Alcántara, *Modernizing Mexican Agriculture: Socio-economic Implications of Technological Change, 1940–1970* (Geneva: U.N. Research Institute for Social Development, 1976).

16 The private business sector was excluded from this compulsory incorporation into the official party, although it was required by law to establish a nation-wide organization.

later years. The organization provided by Cárdenas set up the mechanisms by which class conflicts would be absorbed and transformed within the state.

In addition to establishing the basis for political control and legitimacy, the Cárdenas years also witnessed the expansion of the state's role in the economy. The role of state-owned companies (parastates) expanded as did the state's role in the financial sector. The railways were nationalized, to be administered by a state corporation, and in 1934 the state electrical enterprise, CFE (the Federal Electricity Commission), was set up.

But by far the most important expropriation was that of the British- and American-owned petroleum companies in 1938 and the establishment of the state enterprise *Petróleos Mexicanos* (PEMEX). PEMEX was to carry out exploration, production, refining and, beginning in 1940, the marketing of oil and gas. The expropriation was an extremely popular measure. For most Mexicans it was an act that fulfilled an important revolutionary goal: it allowed Mexicans to gain control of one of the country's most important natural resources, petroleum. The foreign-owned oil companies represented the hated Porfiriato that the revolution had sought to abolish. Porfirio Díaz had had close ties with British and American oil men and had granted them generous privileges to invest in Mexico. In addition these foreign companies paid Mexicans less than foreign workers, even when doing the same job. Moreover, the oil companies were believed to be sending their profits out of the country and were failing to adequately reinvest in exploration and drilling. Finally, the fact that the oil companies consistently opposed Mexico's claim to subsoil rights, established in the 1917 Constitution, aroused nationalist sentiment against them. Coinciding with the nationalist and revolutionary aspirations of the majority of Mexicans, the petroleum nationalization has a central place in Mexican nationalism and in Mexican revolutionary ideology; it undoubtedly played an important role in consolidating support for the regime.[17]

---

17 Good accounts of the oil expropriation are found in J. Richard Powell, *The Mexican Petroleum Industry, 1938–1950* (New York: Russell and Russell, 1972); Antonio J. Bermúdez, *The Mexican National Petroleum Industry* (Stanford: Stanford University Press, 1963); and Richard B. Manke, *Mexican Oil and Natural Gas* (New York: Praeger, 1979).

During the Cárdenas years, the expanding role of public development banks generated the funds required for public-sector investment. Especially important were the financial agencies created for the rural sector, such as the Banco Nacional de Crédito Ejidal (the Bank of Ejidal Credit) and the Banco Nacional de Commercio Exterior (the National Foreign Trade Bank). During the Cárdenas years Nafinsa expanded its activities from real estate loans to a more active role in promoting industry.[18]

The vigorous state action of the period met with increasing opposition from the fledgling private sector that the state itself had created. This resistance, combined with the deteriorating economic situation for which the private sector was in part responsible, precipitated a readjustment within the power structure of the state which gave greater weight to the right wing of the political elite. The private sector was firmly opposed to the Cárdenista economic program and social reforms. Beginning in 1936 this opposition, led by the very conservative Monterrey group, showed their displeasure with government policy by disinvestment, demonstrations, and the suspension of business activities.[19] By 1937 the situation was further exacerbated by an economic recession in the United States, declining silver and oil prices, and the need to import food due to the dislocation caused by the agrarian reform. In addition the expropriation of the petroleum industry and the resultant lack of trained personnel, equipment, and markets produced a sharp decline in oil revenues.[20] In the last two years of Cárdenas' term, inflation increased as did the public deficit. With growing hostility from the private sector, capital flight accelerated. There was downward pressure on the peso and a drain of reserves.

The deepening economic crisis and the opposition from the private sector occasioned a shift to the right within the state as the private sector and its political allies pushed for the abandonment of Cárdenismo. In the face of the growing hostility of the private

---

18 Calvin P. Blair, '*Nacional Financiera*: Entrepreneurship in a Mixed Economy,' in Raymond Vernon, ed., *Public Policy and Private Enterprise in Mexico*, p. 210.
19 See, Juan M. Martínez Nava, *Conflicto estado empresarios* (México, D.F.: Editorial Nueva Imagen, 1984), p. 88.
20 The foreign oil companies retaliated by instituting a blockade against Mexican petroleum.

sector, Cárdenas tried repeatedly to conciliate the bourgeoisie, abandoning his chosen successor as candidate for the presidency, Francisco Múgica, in favor of the more conservative candidacy of Manuel Avila Camacho. The guiding principal for Cárdenas and those in charge of the state was that the institutional order be maintained and that power be transferred peacefully.

In subsequent years, the party–state structure established by Cárdenas became a mechanism of popular containment and control. Labor militancy was dampened as later administrations used the party to coopt both it and peasant militants. The onset of the Second World War created the context for the tight control of labor unions, allowing the administration to extract commitments from labor that there would be no strike activity. Radical labor leaders such as Vicente Lombardo Toledano were replaced by more acquiescent ones. Power was further concentrated in the hands of the presidency as control of the party, Congress, and unions was tightened. Through a system of patronage, labor–government relations became characterized by *charismo*, which is domination by union leaders who use their position to amass political influence, great personal wealth, and power at the expense of their rank and file.[21] The evolution of the party as a mechanism of authoritarian political control was reflected in its change of name in 1946 from the Party of the Mexican Revolution (PRM) to the Institutional Revolutionary Party (PRI). As control over the worker and peasant sectors was consolidated, ties between the state and the private sector increased. The stage was set for a model of development that would benefit Mexico's industrialists while deepening social and economic inequalities.

Roots of Economic Disequilibrium: State-Led Industrialization, 1940–1970

The institutional mechanisms of political incorporation and con-

---

21 On this see, Howard Handleman, 'The Politics of Labor Protest in Mexico,' *Journal of Interamerican Studies and World Affairs* 18, no. 3 (August 1976). The term 'charro' (literally 'cowboy') has its origins in the nickname given to an early leader of the Mexican railroad workers, Luis Gomez Zepeda, who was removed from office due to the embezzlement of union funds.

trol established during the Cárdenas years, combined with the immensely popular reformist measures taken during that sexenio, made possible a period of politically stable peripheral capitalist growth between 1940 and the late 1960s. The model, however, entailed increasing inequalities both in relative and absolute terms —a rising public deficit, a chronic balance of payments problem, and an increasing recourse to foreign borrowing.

Whereas President Cárdenas' economic program had placed heavy emphasis on the agricultural sector, in particular upon small and ejidal agriculture, the post-1940 administrations carried forth an enthusiastic program of import-substitution industrialization, which began by encouraging the domestic manufacture of light consumer goods, and had as its objective the eventual domestic production of intermediate and finally capital goods. Agricultural policy, given considerable attention during the 1930s, would now focus on commercial agricultural export to the neglect of the small peasant and ejidal sector. After 1960 agriculture in general tended to be neglected by public policy. Land redistribution declined markedly after 1940, and what lands were distributed tended to be of poor quality.

The state continued its activist role in the economy. Its primary goal was a high growth rate through industrialization. The instruments of state intervention established in the earlier period were now put to full use in the project of state-led industrialization. The Second World War, producing a shortage of imported consumer products, gave further impetus to the government's industrialization program. In 1941 the first Law of Manufacturing Industries was passed; it provided tax exemptions for new industries for five years. In that same year sweeping legislative changes laid the basis for the readjustment of the banking system necessary for the new economic project. The Banco de México received new authority to vary reserve requirements, alter discount policy, and to buy, sell, and hold securities.[22] Particularly after 1960 the manipulation of reserve requirements became an important mechanism by which the

---

22 On this see David H. Shelton, 'The Banking System: Money and the Goal of Growth,' in Raymond Vernon, ed., *Public Policy and Private Enterprise in Mexico*, p. 151.

state was able to finance noninflationary growth. New legislation also made it possible for the state to direct the private-banking sector in the amounts it could lend to various activities. Hence, both state and private-sector credit could be directed toward areas considered by the government to be of priority. Between 1940 and 1960, the banking system channeled credit particularly toward industry but also toward commercial agriculture. After 1960 the bias toward industry became even more marked: whereas in 1960 industry received three times the credit that agriculture did, by 1972 it was receiving four times the amount received by agriculture.[23]

Nafinsa was reorganized and strengthened to become a full-scale development bank. Its Ley Orgánica (December 1940) emphasized Nafinsa's industrial-promotion role, calling for it to promote investment in industrial enterprises, to regulate the securities market, and to provide long-term credits. Especially after 1947, when the chairman of Nafinsa's board of directors became the secretary of finance, Nafinsa became an important instrument of executive policymaking. But while Nafinsa stimulated the establishment of many new enterprises, its investment in infrastructure was of fundamental importance. Between 1953 and 1961 the share of total resources going to infrastructure never fell below 50 percent as the government strove to break bottlenecks presented by transportation, communications, and electricity.[24] Private *financieras* (industrial investment banks) also became tools for industrial promotion, having been given the authority to issue securities for sale to the public and becoming partners in industrial enterprises. Other mechanisms to encourage industry included substantial protection through tariff and quota restrictions that many observers regarded as excessive.[25]

23 Manuel Gallás and Adalberto García Rocha, 'El desarrollo económico reciente de México,' in James W. Wilkie et al., eds., *Contemporary Mexico* (Los Angeles: UCLA Latin American Center, 1976), p. 415.

24 Calvin P. Blair, '*Nacional Financiera*: Entrepreneurship in a Mixed Economy,' in Raymond Vernon, ed., *Public Policy and Private Enterprise in Mexico*, pp. 223–224.

25 René Villarreal, 'The Policy of Import Substituting Industrialization, 1929–1975,' in José Luis Reyna and Richard S. Weinert, eds., *Authoritarianism in Mexico* (Philadelphia: Institute for the Study of Human Issues, 1977), p. 73; Rafael Izquierdo, 'Protectionism in Mexico,' in Raymond Vernon, ed., *Public Policy and Private Enterprise in Mexico*.

The expansion of parastate activity, although often seen as a threat by private-sector entrepreneurs, stimulated the expansion of the private sector and guaranteed high profits through the provision of cheap energy and inputs. Under President Miguel Alemán Valdés (1946–1952) PEMEX's efficiency was improved. To demonstrate the growing importance of the parastates, consider that by the 1950s investment by parastates was larger than that of the federal government.[26]

The state's central role in economic development naturally entailed ever-increasing state spending. The expenditure of the public sector grew in absolute and relative terms during the period. Total expenditure of the public sector as a percentage of GDP increased from 11.5 percent in 1940 to 23 percent in 1967.[27] The state's investment role increased steadily throughout the period. Between 1950 and 1970 the public sector accounted for 30 percent of the country's aggregate investment.[28]

Although industrialization was the state's top priority, the 1940–1960 period witnessed important state-supported development in the agriculture commercial exports which was using increasingly capital-intensive methods. The agricultural sector supported expanding industrialism by providing cheap food for the urban population and by providing the foreign exchange necessary for imported industrial inputs. Incentives for commercial-export agriculture included massive irrigation projects and green-revolution technology, most of which occurred in northern and northwest Mexico. Meanwhile small and ejidal agriculture was left to stagnate: the proportion of *ejidatarios* (ejido members) receiving credit from the government fell from 30 percent in 1936 to 14 percent in 1960.[29] Although these policies sacrificed the small and ejidal producer, they created an acceleration in agricultural production. Between 1946 and 1956 agriculture grew at the rate of 7.6 percent annually, a rate above

26 Miguel S. Wionczek, 'Incomplete Formal Planning: Mexico,' in Everett E. Hagen, ed., *Planning Economic Development* (Homewood, IL: Richard D. Irwin, 1963), p. 155.

27 Brian Griffiths, *Mexican Monetary Policy and Economic Development* (New York: Praeger, 1972), p. 48.

28 Roger Hansen, *The Politics of Mexican Development* (Baltimore: Johns Hopkins University Press, 1980), p. 210.

29 Ibid., p. 83.

that of the total national product.[30] Mexico not only became self-sufficient in food by the mid-1960s, but by 1955 cotton, coffee, and sugar represented 30 percent of total exports, replacing the traditional mineral exports of gold, silver, and zinc.[31]

As with other Latin American countries, however, by the early 1950s the government's economic model was running into difficulties, as the easy import-substitution stage—the production of light consumer goods that had previously been imported—came to a close. Further growth was blocked due to the narrowness of the domestic consumer market. Moreover, the state-led development model was, by the mid-1950s, generating considerable inflation due to the fact that up to this point development had been largely financed by increasing the money supply.[32] Following the conventional wisdom of the day, the government took measures to attract foreign capital, stimulate industrialization, and abandon inflationary financing. This new strategy—known as 'stabilizing development,' implemented between 1958 and 1970—sought economic growth with price stability. The objective of state policy, to make the transition to import substitution in intermediate and capital goods, was to be carried out with private capital, both domestic and foreign. Hence, from the 1950s onward, public investment priorities emphasized transportation and industry even more heavily. Agriculture was now dangerously neglected. Agricultural credit as a share of total credit decreased from 15 percent in 1960 to 9 percent in 1970.[33] The effort to stimulate industrialization brought with it increasing foreign investment. Between 1950 and 1970 foreign investment increased five times, installing itself largely in manufacturing, especially in the fastest-growing economic sectors.[34]

Moreover, in the 1950s the government began to rely on

---

30 Leopoldo Solís, *La realidad económica mexicana: Retrovisión y perspectivas*, p. 96.
31 William O. Freithaler, *Mexico's Foreign Trade and Economic Development* (New York: Praeger, 1968), p. 85.
32 Between 1950 and 1954, for example, the quantity of money increased 17.8 percent per year. Manuel Gallás and Adalberto García Rocha, 'El desarrollo económico reciente de México,' in James W. Wilkie et al., *Contemporary Mexico*, p. 411.
33 Leopoldo Solís, *La realidad económica mexicana: Retrovisión y perspectivas*, p. 12.
34 Richard S. Weinert, 'Foreign Capital in Mexico,' in Susan Kaufman Purcell, ed., *Mexican–United States Relations* (New York: Praeger, 1981), p. 117.

foreign borrowing in order to finance investment without generating inflation. After the 1950s, financial authorities began to introduce high rates of reserve requirements in the banking system to help finance public expenditure. Interest rates were also raised to increase the volume of domestic savings. But the government also sought to supplement internal sources as the financial system proved less and less capable of providing the public sector's expanding investment needs. Mexico's public foreign debt, according to Rosario Green, 'became the adjustment mechanism through which the Mexican government filled the gap between public income, on the one hand, and public investment and expenditure, on the other.'[35] Hence Mexico's debt-service ratio increased from 16.3 percent in 1960 to 23.2 percent in 1970.[36] President Díaz Ordaz inherited in 1964 a foreign debt 150 percent higher than that inherited by the previous administration six years earlier.[37] During this early period foreign financing, which began to take on increasing importance, came largely from official sources.[38]

Recourse to foreign borrowing was in part, at least, made necessary because of the low rate of taxation on the private sector—an arrangement felt to be necessary to stimulate industrial expansion. Attempts at tax reform during the 1960s were largely ineffectual due to the vigorous opposition of the private sector. In fact, those changes that were made during the 1960s had a further regressive impact, producing an increase in the share of taxes coming from labor income.[39]

---

35 Maria del Rosario Green, 'Mexico's Economic Dependence,' in ibid, p. 106.
36 Robert E. Looney, *Mexico's Economy: A Policy Analysis and Forecasts to 1990* (Boulder, CO: Westview Press, 1978), p. 17.
37 E. V. K. Fitzgerald, 'The State and Capital Accumulation in Mexico,' *Journal of Latin American Studies* 10, no. 2 (November 1978): 33.
38 It has been suggested that the impact of high reserve requirements was higher interest rates and a tightening of credit for private investment. This made necessary more state expenditure as 'the state acts as the last resort in the face of declining private investment.' Bennett and Sharpe, 'The State as Banker and Entrepreneur: The Last Resort Character of the Mexican State's Intervention,' in Sylvia Ann Hewlett and Richard S. Weinert, eds., *Brazil and Mexico: Patterns in Late Development* (Philadelphia: Institute for the Study of Human Issues, 1982), p. 201. This has been disputed by E. V. K. Fitzgerald, 'The State and Capital Accumulation in Mexico,' p. 276.
39 Leopoldo Solís, *La realidad económica mexicana: Retrovisión y perspectivas*, p. 25.

Although ostensibly the period of stabilizing development was a success insofar as it achieved steady growth rates without inflation, there were a number of underlying problems that became increasingly apparent by the mid- to late 1960s. Economic growth had begun to stagnate. There had been a persistently unfavorable balance of trade in merchandise since 1940. Between 1950 and 1970—with the exception of 1955—the current account had been in deficit.[40] The problem became especially grave between 1965 and 1970 when the balance of payments deficit went from $367 million to $946 million (U.S. dollar values).[41] Unemployment and underemployment in the late 1960s have been estimated at between 40 and 50 percent.[42] Economic inequality had since 1940 increased both in relative and absolute terms. The roots of the economic stagnation that Mexico began to experience from the mid-1960s are to be found, to a large extent, in the economic model so enthusiastically implemented by the government. Public policy's neglect of the agricultural sector began to impact negatively upon Mexico's balance of payments. Although between 1960 and 1970 the value of agricultural exports was increasing in absolute terms, agriculture's proportion of the value of total exports declined from 63.9 to 54.8 percent.[43] And whereas between 1960 and 1970 agricultural production grew on average 3.6 percent per year, between 1965 and 1970 it grew at the rate of only 1 percent per year, far below population growth. The stage was set for Mexico to become a net food importer by the early 1970s.

Because the import-substitution strategy had been an internally oriented one, measures had not been taken to stimulate the exportation of Mexican manufactured goods. Protection from foreign imports, which shifted to quota protection in the 1960s, encouraged the maintenance of an inefficient manufacturing

40 Brian Griffiths, *Mexican Monetary Policy and Economic Development*, p. 41.
41 Clark W. Reynolds, 'Porque el "desarrollo estabilizador" de Mexico fue en realidad destabilizador,' in *El trimestre económico* 44, núm. 4 (Octubre–Diciembre 1977): 1001.
42 Carlos Tello, *La política económica en México, 1970–1976* (México, D.F.: Siglo XXI, 1980), p. 76.
43 Emilio Leyva, 'Burguesía agrícola y dependencia,' in Ramiro Reyes Esparza et al., eds., *La burguesía mexicana*, 3d ed. (México, D.F.: Editorial Nuestro Tiempo, 1978), pp. 105, 108.

sector that had difficulty competing internationally. Nor were there subsidies or tax exemptions to encourage the exportation of manufactured goods. While exports stagnated, however, the minimum imports required for the continued functioning of the productive apparatus were increasing. Although the objective of economic policy had been to make the transition to import substitution of intermediate and capital goods, Mexico in fact remained highly dependent on the importation of capital goods. The import substitution that had occurred during the 1960s had promoted the manufacture of consumer durables, the market for which was becoming saturated. While durable consumer goods decreased their relative share in total imports, imports of machinery and equipment increased their share from 23 percent in 1940 to 36 percent in 1970.[44] Policy, in fact, had protected final consumer goods considerably more than intermediate and capital goods. Mexico was trapped in the typical Latin American dilemma in which economic expansion depends on the ability to import but exports were not expanding rapidly enough.

The social implications of the economic model were also typically Latin American: rural unemployment, rapid rural–urban migration, and a burgeoning urban lumpenproletariat. General neglect of the small peasant and ejidal agricultural sectors and an emphasis on capital-intensive commercial-export agriculture had produced unemployment in the countryside and increasing rural–urban migration. Industrial policy, which had encouraged the use of capital-intensive methods through the liberal importation of capital goods, had produced an industrialism that was incapable of absorbing the expanding urban labor force. Measures to stimulate foreign investment, far from solving Mexico's development dilemma—as originally envisioned— were exacerbating the balance of payments disequilibrium. By the late 1960s, net payments abroad in the form of profit remittances and payment of interest on external private and public debt were worsening the foreign exchange problem.[45]

The industrialization process produced increasing private-

---

44 Leopoldo Solís, *La realidad económica mexicana: Retrovisión y perspectivas*, p. 7.
45 Robert E. Looney, *Mexico's Economy: A Policy Analysis and Forecasts to 1990*, p. 16.

sector concentration. Between 1960 and 1970 there emerged powerful financial–industrial groups—major industrial firms tied in with one of the ten or so major banks. Indeed, by 1968 two banking groups controlled 51 percent of the capital reserves and 72 percent of the total resources of the private sector.[46]

The deteriorating economic situation placed increasing strains on the political system starting from the mid-1960s. Indeed, even as early as 1958 the official labor movement was demanding substantial increases in minimum wages. Labor reaction against both charrismo and the containment of wages were producing independent unions among the railway workers, teachers, and peasants. Land invasions began to occur with increasing frequency from 1958 on. President López Mateos' (1958–1964) formula of 'left within the revolution' and 'balanced revolution', even as superficial as it was, met stiff resistance from the private business sector. An increase in land redistribution and social welfare spending, a foreign policy defending Cuba, and electoral reform reflected López Mateos' attempt to placate leftist pressure. But opposition to even these mildly reformist measures mounted, and the government's response toward dissident groups became increasingly authoritarian and repressive. Clearly, from the mid-1950s on, the state was becoming less reluctant to use violence to quell unrest and more rigid in its suspicion of dissenters. The government had responded to the railway workers' demands for increased wages in 1958 by forcing the workers back to work and by arresting and imprisoning thousands of workers. Although the level of violence exerted against the doctors' strike (1964–1965) was less, reprisals in the form of arrests and firings occurred.[47] Student disturbances during the 1950s and 1960s were usually put down with government troops. Deeper attempts at democratization had clearly been rejected, as demonstrated by the failure of Carlos Madrazo—president of the PRI Central Committee during the administration of Díaz Ordaz (1964–1965)—to introduce a system of primary elections that would have democratized the Party. Madrazo's

46 Alonso Aquilar M. and Fernando Carmona, *México: Riqueza y Miseria* (México, D.F.: Editorial Nuestre Tiempo, S.A., 1972), p. 220.
47 Good accounts of these events are found in Evelyn Stevens, *Protest and Response in Mexico* (Cambridge, MA: MIT Press, 1974).

efforts caused considerable discomfort among more conservative elements of the Party; removed from his Party post in 1965, he died under mysterious circumstances in an airplane crash in 1969. The climax of the mounting unrest and escalating government repression occurred in 1968 with the student strike and massacre at Tlatelolco of an estimated two hundred students by government troops.

The student movement of 1968 and its violent aftermath marked a turning point in Mexican politics. It was no ordinary protest movement concerned with narrow professional goals. Its objectives embodied protest of a more generalized political, social, and economic nature: a demand that Mexican politics be democratized, and a call for an end to social and economic injustice.[48] The violence with which the government met the student protest seriously undermined the regime's legitimacy and precipitated further opposition in the form of increases in rural guerrilla insurgency and leftist criticism of the government.

Conclusions

By the late 1960s the Mexican state faced a serious economic and political crisis. The development model it had been pursuing contained bottlenecks that state policy was unable to overcome. The emergence of a powerful private sector created by the state itself presented an important political obstacle to government policies—such as tax reform and reforms and incentives in the agricultural sector—that could have alleviated the situation. Moreover, the authoritarian political system was becoming increasingly rigid in the face of growing social and political unrest. But the depth of the legitimacy crisis engendered by the government's violent reaction to social protest strengthened the reformists within the state and gave rise to a new strategy: called 'shared development,' it represented an attempt to return Mexican public policy to its populist origins. As the economy deterio-

---

48 Yoram Shapira, 'Mexico: The Impact of the 1968 Student Protest on Echeverría's Reformism,' *Journal of Inter-American Studies and World Affairs* 19, no. 4 (November 1977): 562.

rated and as the class struggle heated up, the debate over 'solutions' increased within the state. As we shall see, the state became less and less capable of containing conflict, reproducing within itself the contradictory urges for reform and repression.

3

Genesis of Policy Change: From Shared Development to the Petroleum Export Strategy

The Economic Program of Shared Development: Welfare and Investment

The deteriorating economic situation of the late 1960s and the trauma of 1968 caused Mexico's political leadership to reassess Mexico's economic model along with its increasingly closed political system. The traditional goal of stabilizing development was now criticized both within and outside the government for its single-minded emphasis on industrial growth; for its neglect of agriculture in general and small and ejidal agriculture in particular; and for its disregard for social justice.[1] The new program espoused by the administration of President Luis Echeverría became known as 'shared development.' While in the political sphere it aimed to 'open up' the political system, in the realm of economic policy it placed emphasis on redistributive and social welfare measures and a commitment to improve the agricultural sector, especially small and ejidal agriculture. Echeverría's economic program also aimed to increase state investment in order to remove the bottlenecks to economic growth.

The new project was by no means unanimously supported by state managers. The strongest supporters of the economic pro-

---

1 On the growing criticism of the old stabilizing-development model within the bureaucracy, see Merilee S. Grindle, *Bureaucrats, Politicians and Peasants in Mexico* (Berkeley: University of California Press, 1979).

[45]

gram of shared-development were found in the Ministries of the Presidency and of Natural Resources and Industrial Development, while the Ministry of Finance and Public Credit (henceforth referred to as the Ministry of Finance) and the Central Bank, sharing similar views with the private sector, clung to the old formula of stabilizing development. Powerful members of the private sector also held strong reservations on the question of greater tolerance of political dissidents, sharing an affinity of views with old-guard political and union leaders. With strong opposition to shared development both within and outside of the state, policy during the period continually vacillated as the president responded to the competing pressures of those who, on the one hand, felt his reform did not go far enough and those who, on the other, feared that his program veered too far to the left. While economic policy vacillated between orthodox restrictions and populist redistribution, attempts to foster a democratic opening alternated with outright repression.

Initially, Echeverría's approach to Mexico's economic troubles was a conservative one. Faced with a severe balance of payments problem and inflation, Echeverría became convinced of the efficacy of the usual belt-tightening recommendations made by the finance ministry. Hence, public expenditure was budgeted at a very low level for 1971, with a drastic cut in public investment. The government also reduced its external borrowing to help correct the deteriorating balance of payments situation. But the government's restrictive spending policy exacerbated the normal fall in economic activity that accompanies the beginning of each administration, and a recession was produced. Although inflation was controlled and the balance of payments deficit reduced, the GDP per capita actually fell in 1971.[2] While the economy stagnated and unemployment rose, the Central Bank's annual report indicated the accumulation of substantial reserves. The combination of a seemingly induced economic recession and

---

2 E. V. K. Fitzgerald, 'Stabilization Policy in Mexico: The Fiscal Deficit and Macroeconomic Equilibrium, 1960–1977,' in Rosemary Thorpe and Laurence Whitehead, eds., *Inflation and Stabilization in Latin America* (London: Macmillan, 1979), p. 40.

the accumulation of reserves brought about the discrediting of the finance secretary and gave increased credence to those state managers who were advising an economic program of shared development.[3] The proponents of shared development argued that it was only through increased state spending and major tax reform that the presidential objectives of improved income distribution and the removal of investment bottlenecks blocking economic growth could be achieved. Hence, the new expenditure program (at least as originally conceived) was not simply a social-welfare spending spree to recoup support from the popular classes; it was believed that the failure of past governments to invest created a need for greater investments during the 1970s to 'catch up.'

Total government spending—current and capital accounts, including the parastates whose budgets were controlled by the federal government—increased from 23.6 percent of GDP in 1970 to 36.6 percent of GDP in 1975.[4] Expenditure was increased on such items as health, housing, and education. The social security system was expanded, and the National Workers Housing Fund Institution (INFONAVIT), financed by a tax on business, was set up to provide low-cost housing for workers. Equally important, however, was the dramatic increase in public investment. As a proportion of total investment, public investment went from 35.5 percent in 1970 to 46.2 percent in 1975.[5] The government's efforts to remove the bottlenecks restricting further growth is demonstrated by the increasing public investment going into agriculture, energy, and heavy-industrial and capital goods. In the agricultural sector, public policy was geared toward the achievement of agricultural self-sufficiency and toward alleviating the plight of the small and ejidal farmer. Of total government expenditure, agriculture went from 7.5 percent in 1971 to 14.7 percent

---

3 See Leopoldo Solís, *Economic Policy Reform in Mexico* (New York: Pergamon, 1981), p. 52 ff. Solís—head of the Economic Programing Directorate of the Ministry of the Presidency between 1971 and 1975— provides a very good account of the economic policy debates of the period.

4 C. Gribomont and M. Rimez, 'La política económica del gobierno de Luis Echeverría (1971–1976): Un primer ensayo de interpretación,' in *El trimestre económico* 44, vol. 4, núm. 176 (Octubre–Diciembre 1977): 784.

5 Ibid., p. 787.

in 1975, while industry's and commerce's proportion remained stable at around 30 percent during the period.[6]

Small peasant and ejidal agriculture was favored through a number of measures: favoritism was shown toward cooperatives in the granting of credit and irrigated land, guaranteed prices were established for farm products and intermediaries were eliminated—especially through the expansion of CONASUPO (National Company of Popular Goods), a state marketing board that sought to supply basic foodstuffs to the poor—while the number of agricultural schools was expanded.[7] Measures were taken to restore ejidal lands to their original owners, and land was purchased to create additional ejidos.

A concerted effort was made to stimulate manufacturing exports. Import duties were reduced to improve the competitiveness of Mexican manufactured goods, and direct subsidies were made available for exports as were credits at low rates of interest from the newly formed IMCE (Mexican Institute of Foreign Trade). An attempt was also made to restructure import protection so as to provide greater stimulus to the domestic manufacture of capital goods. The administration also pursued a vigorous policy to stimulate the establishment of *maquiladoras* or assembly plants.[8]

The parastate sector grew rapidly during the Echeverría years. By 1975 almost 50 percent of the total expenditure of the federal government (capital and current) went to state enterprises.[9] The most important parastate investments occurred in PEMEX, CFE

6 Ibid., p. 786.
7 On Echeverría's economic program, see especially Steven E. Sanderson, *Agrarian Populism and the Mexican State* (Berkeley: University of California Press, 1981); and Merilee S. Grindle, *Bureaucrats, Politicians and Peasants in Mexico* (Berkeley: University of California Press, 1977).
8 Mainly in such sectors as electrical articles and electromechanical items, foreign firms establishing within twenty kilometers of the Mexican–American border were allowed, by legislation passed in 1971, to freely import needed inputs, provided that they export. In 1972 these firms were allowed to establish anywhere in the country. See C. Gribomont and M. Rimez, 'La política económica del gobierno de Luis Echeverría (1971–1976): Un primer ensayo de interpretación,' p. 821.
9 E. V. K. Fitzgerald, *Patterns of Saving and Investment in Mexico* (Cambridge: Cambridge University Press, 1977), p. 9. Salvador Cordero, 'Estado y burguesía en la decada de 1970,' in Jorge Alonso, Coord., *El Estado Mexicano* (México, D.F.: Editorial Nueva Imagen, 1982), p. 66.

(the Federal Commission of Electricity), and FERTIMEX (the National Fertilizer Company); together these entities accounted for 90 percent of government parastate investment by 1977.[10] Although increases were made in the prices charged by parastates, especially in the areas of electricity and gas in 1972 and 1974, these increases were not sufficient to halt their growing deficits. Indeed, the deficit in the current accounts of those parastates whose budgets were controlled by the federal government absorbed more than 50 percent of the savings of the public sector in 1974–1975.[11]

The Failure of Shared Development

Despite an upsurge in economic activity in 1972, Echeverría's shared-development strategy had failed miserably by 1976. The reforms in agriculture had not had the effects intended: during the period 1970–1976 agriculture grew at the rate of only 1.6 percent and between 1975 and 1976 the volume of output actually fell; between 1971 and 1976 the deficit in the current account of the balance of payments quadrupled.[12] With declining exports and heavy import needs due to the government's ambitious investment program, the state was forced to rely on foreign borrowing. During the six years of shared development, the foreign debt grew in U.S. dollars from $4.5 billion to $19.6 billion.[13] The public deficit rose in Mexican pesos from 4.8 billion to 42 billion between 1971 and 1975.[14] Inflation increased, especially

10 Luis Angeles, *Crisis y coyuntura de la economía mexicana* (México, D.F.: Editorial El Caballito, 1979), p. 83. In Mexico there are twelve wholly state-owned enterprises whose budgets are controlled by the federal government. In 1982, the government owned a majority of shares in approximately 300 other enterprises.
11 Octavio Gómez G., 'Las empresas públicas en México: Desempeño riciente y relaciones con la política económico,' in *El trimestre económico* 49, núm. 2 (Abril–Junio 1982): 456.
12 Robert E. Looney, *Mexico's Economy: A Policy Analysis and Forecasts to 1990* (Boulder, CO: Westview Press, 1978), p. 69.
13 George W. Grayson, *The United States and Mexico: Patterns of Influence* (New York: Praeger, 1984), p. 54.
14 Robert E. Looney, *Mexico's Economy: A Policy Analysis and Forecasts to 1990*, p. 68.

after 1973, as did capital flight. In 1976 the GDP grew by only 4.2 percent, slightly more than the population. In October of 1976, Mexico was forced to reach a politically unpopular agreement with the International Monetary Fund (IMF) in return for a loan of $1 billion.

The worsening economic situation between 1970 and 1976 stemmed from the interplay between international economic events and a growing internal economic crisis that faced political obstacles to its resolution in the form of growing opposition from the private sector and mounting popular unrest. Between 1965 and 1971 difficulties occurred in international financial relations with the growing uncertainty of the principal foreign currencies. When in 1971 the United States, faced with economic stagnation and an overvalued currency, ended the free convertibility of the dollar to gold, the North American dollar experienced a devaluation of 10 percent. The disruption in the international financial system precipitated inflation and stagnation in the industrialized countries, as each took measures to rectify its balance of payments situation by discouraging imports. The United States took measures that made access to the American market more difficult. In 1971 Nixon's 10 percent surcharge on imports shattered Mexico's hopes of increasing exports, especially those of manufactured products. The general slowdown in the American economy also caused a drop in demand for Mexican goods, whose exports were further discouraged by the maintenance of an overvalued peso. Declining American tourism also negatively affected Mexico's balance of payments. And the world food crisis of 1972 worsened the crisis of Mexican agriculture, making food self-sufficiency there a top priority.

Mexico was also hit hard by the 1973 oil crisis. A past policy of low prices and minimal investment in the petroleum sector during the stabilizing-development period had rendered Mexico ill prepared to face the world oil shortage. Hence, in 1971, Mexico was for the first time a net importer of petroleum, another factor impacting badly on Mexico's balance of payments situation. At the same time, the presence of recycled petroleum dollars in the international banking system made it possible for Echeverría to borrow readily on the international market. While the slowdown in the American economy rendered the United States less able to purchase Mexican goods, American banks had a surplus of funds for which they had little demand. Hence, almost unlimited credit was made available to the administration of Echeverría.

Expanding the foreign debt increasingly became the way out for an administration faced with the perceived need to rapidly expand government expenditures while unable to implement basic tax reform. Fundamental changes in the tax system had been planned to help provide the funds necessary to make shared development possible. Tax reform, however, was successfully blocked by the united opposition of the business sector and their bureaucratic allies in the Central Bank.[15] Four attempts were made during Echeverría's administration to establish tax reform—in 1971, 1972, and two in 1975—all of which were either considerably watered down or blocked by the private sector.[16] As a result of these tax reform efforts, the government's income increased only slightly. The reforms that were achieved were too little too late. It has been suggested that had the full fiscal reform been carried out as originally intended, the public deficit could have been kept in check while the rising rate of real national income would have generated the necessary surplus of private savings to finance the deficit.[17]

President Echeverría's conflict with the private sector over tax

15 While the Office of the Presidency supported a thorough reform, the Finance Ministry supported reform with qualifications. Leopoldo Solís, *Economic Policy Reform in Mexico*, p. 75.

16 The 1971 Fiscal Reform Bill's original aim was to increase tax rates for upper-income groups but, because of pressure from the private sector, it affected them only marginally. The 1972 reform was to affect incomes from rents, investment, and capital assets. It was dropped following meetings with the private sector. The 1975 reform taxed luxury items and middle-income groups more heavily, but again it avoided measures that would have disturbed the confidence of the private sector. Resistance from the private sector got the luxury tax reduced from 10 to 7 percent. Also, in 1975, government plans for integral tax reform—which would have included a tax on value-added, and on resources, agriculture, and livestock, along with a program to combat tax evasion—was not put forward due to entrepreneurial opposition. On this see Leopoldo Solís, *Economic Policy Reform in Mexico*; and Juan M. Nava Martínez, *Conflicto estado empresarios* (México, D.F.: Editorial Nueva Imagen, 1984), pp. 194–195.

17 E. V. K. Fitzgerald, 'Stabilization Policy in Mexico: The Fiscal Deficit and Macroeconomic Equilibrium, 1960–1967,' p. 42. In Rosemary Thorpe and Laurence Whitehead, eds., *Inflation and Stabilization in Latin America*, Tax reform, however, does not solve the problem of a foreign-exchange shortage.

reform was but one issue among many that precipitated a deterioration of relations between the state and private interests. This deterioration was reflected in the increasingly large capital flight that began in 1973, putting severe downward pressure on the peso. The early years of Echeverría's administration were seemingly characterized by cordial relations between business and the state—or at least the absence of systematic opposition from the private sector. By 1973, however, there were a number of state actions that were causing the private sector some distress. The dramatic increase in government expenditure from 1972, the expansion of the activities of parastates, and the increasing intervention of the state in the economy were of growing concern to the private sector. Complaints that government spending fueled inflation, of extravagance and waste in the public sector, were a recurring refrain that became ever-more persistent as the sexenio wore on. Redistributive measures taken during the period, including healthy wage increases and price controls, were all vigorously opposed by the private sector. Echeverría's more nationalistic policies were not liked either. The private sector opposed, for example, measures to control direct foreign investment on the grounds that they would hurt the investment climate.[18] Echeverría's leftist rhetoric was no doubt also an important factor in the private sector's loss of confidence.

The private sector blamed the rising level of political violence in the country on Echeverría's tolerance for leftist activities. The assassination of prominent businessman Eugenio Garza Sada by guerrillas produced a virulent attack against Echeverría and a hardening of entrepreneurial opposition. In 1975 the major entrepreneurial organizations established the CCE, the Coordinating Entrepreneurial Council, which espoused an ideology of individualism and private property.[19] The CCE pressured the

18 Gary Gereffi and Peter Evans, 'Transnational Corporations, Dependent Development and State Policy in the Semi-Periphery: A Comparison of Brazil and Mexico,' *Latin American Research Review* 45, no. 3 (1981): 51.

19 The only major entrepreneurial organization not to join the CCE was CANACINTRA—the National Chamber of Manufacturing Industries, representing small and medium industrial firms—which has a history of greater support for state initiatives and state intervention in the economy. On the emergence and attitudes of this group see, Stanford A. Mosk, *Industrial Revolution in Mexico* (Berkeley: University of California Press, 1954).

Echeverría government to abandon its reformist program, criticizing the expansion of the state and calling for privatization. The CCE also supported direct foreign investment that would allow majority foreign control. Entrepreneur–state relations took a new turn for the worse during the last months of 1975 when Echeverría expropriated 4387 hectares of land in Sonora and distributed it among 433 peasants. This action led to work stoppages by the big agricultural farmers; they were joined by the industrialists of Monterrey who had the support of the CCE in their struggle. With land invasions mounting, in his last day in office Echeverría announced that some 405,000 hectares of land would be redistributed in Durango and Sinaloa. This act precipitated another general strike by agriculturalists.

If by 1973 capital flight had become a serious problem, by 1976 it had assumed disastrous proportions: over a half-billion U.S. dollars left the country on the capital account over the winter.[20] With further increases in the current-account deficit, the government had no choice but to borrow abroad.

But if Echeverría's reforms alienated the private sector, they often did not go far enough fast enough for workers and peasants. Indeed, stiff entrepreneurial opposition watered down, if it did not block, reforms that might have assuaged popular demands. There is no question that the agricultural policies that so angered the private sector were a response to the mounting agrarian unrest which characterized the sexenio. Increasing violence and guerrilla activity in the countryside had led to intervention by the army in the early 1960s. By the 1970s a myriad of independent combative organizations were emerging in the ejidos and villages. By the mid-1970s, the pace of peasant land takeovers was rising rapidly and a number of independent peasant organizations had arisen.[21]

Labor unrest also characterized the period as leaders of the major labor organizations demanded price controls and wage increases, especially beginning in 1973. The fall in real wages that

---

20 E. V. K. Fitzgerald, 'Stabilization Policy in Mexico: The Fiscal Deficit and Macroeconomic Equilibrium, 1960–1977,' p. 49.
21 On peasant mobilization during this period, see Sanderson, *Agrarian Populism and the Mexican State*; and in addition, Gustavo Esteva, *The Struggle for Rural Mexico* (South Hadley, MA: Bergin and Garvey Publishers, 1983).

accompanied the 1973 inflation led to worker demands for an emergency increase and threats of a general strike.[22] Between 1973 and 1977, 3600 strikes occurred in response to layoffs, unemployment, rising inflation, and dissatisfaction with *charro* leadership.[23] The movement for democratization within several of the labor unions produced an upsurge of independent unions.

Initially the Echeverría government had attempted to satisfy increasing demands for democratization, to accommodate itself to youth, and to absorb some of the minor political parties that had arisen during the 1960s. It has been suggested that—at the outset, at least—Echeverría supported union democratization, the removal of charro leadership, and the emergence of democratic unions as part of his program for a democratic opening.[24] The Electoral Code of 1973 reduced the voting age from twenty-one to eighteen, while the age requirement for the Chamber of Deputies was reduced from twenty-five to twenty-one and for senators from thirty-five to thirty. In addition the proportion of the popular vote required before a party could be represented in the Chamber of Deputies was reduced from 2.5 to 1.5 percent. Political parties other than the dominant PRI were conceded representation on the Federal Electoral Commission and were granted access to television and radio.[25] Government censorship was loosened, and the 1971 General Amnesty provided for the release of imprisoned leaders of the 1968 student movement.

However, as popular unrest and violence escalated, President Echeverría abandoned this brief democratic opening. The political objectives of shared development failed almost as miserably as did its economic program. Censorship was tightened, a purge of the important daily newspaper *Excélsior* was carried out, and the

22 A strike was averted when the government acceded to the workers' demands for an 18 percent increase.

23 James D. Cockcroft, *Mexico: Class Formation, Capital Accumulation and the State* (New York: Monthly Review Press, 1983), p. 249.

24 Yoram Shapira, 'Mexico: The Impact of the 1968 Student Protest on Echeverría's Reformism,' *Journal of Inter-American Studies and World Affairs* 19, no. 4 (November 1977): 570.

25 However, the detailed procedures that were required for the registration of political parties was a discouraging feature. On Echeverría's electoral reform, see especially Rafael Segovia, 'La reforma política: El ejecutivo federal, el P.R.I. y las elecciones del 1973,' in El Colegio de México, ed., *La vida política en Mexico, 1970–1973* (México, D.F.: El Colegio de méxico, 1974).

government threw its support behind Fidel Velázquez and the old charro leadership. A nationwide strike instigated in 1976 by the electrical workers—the union in which the 'democratic tendency' was centred—was broken up by the army. During the last years of the sexenio, this administration that had flirted briefly with reformism was being pushed relentlessly toward the right.[26]

In the final analysis, the gains achieved by the popular classes during the Echeverría administration were ephemeral. Salary increases succeeded only in slowing the deterioration of workers' pay that occurred during the period.[27] Meanwhile, the rate of profit did not decline and enterprises expanded.[28] Reflecting the crisis of the agricultural sector, the income of rural producers deteriorated faster than that of workers in the urban sector.[29] Increasing migration to urban centers, especially to Mexico City, produced many social problems that continued to plague Mexico.

With the intensification of class conflict in a situation of economic deterioration, the state was becoming less and less capable of implementing any sort of coherent economic program. The state was the captive of the contradictions of the peripheral capitalism that it had been instrumental in creating. Economic stagnation, growing inequality and marginality, and severe social unrest would not allow a return to the restrictive policies of stabilizing development, as the private sector and some state managers were advocating. Nor could the state, given the tremendous growth of the private sector since 1940, attain sufficient autonomy to 'reform' Mexican capitalism. As class conflict heated up—with the state as the object of class struggle—the Mexican political situation became increasingly volatile. The contradictory demands of the participants of that struggle were reflected in the

---

26 Admittedly, the regime had never been ideologically consistent. It was rumored that the 1971 attack by *los Halcones*, a right-wing paramilitary group, against students, had occurred with Echeverría's tacit approval. See Kenneth F. Johnson, *Mexican Democracy: A Critical View* (New York: Praeger, 1978).

27 C. Gribomont and M. Rimez, 'La política económica del gobierno de Luis Echeverría (1970–1976): Un primer ensayo de interpretación,' p. 801.

28 Américo Saldívar, *Ideología y política del estado mexicano (1970–1976)* (Mexico: Siglo XXI, 1980), p. 187.

29 Eugenio Rovzar, 'Análisis de las tendencias en la distributión del ingreso en México (1958–1977),' in Rolando Cordera and Carlos Tello, coords., *La disequalidad en México* (México, D.F.: Siglo XXI, 1984), p. 308.

ambivalence of public policy, which vacillated between reformism and political and economic exclusion of the popular classes. With the exhaustion of their economic strategy, bureaucratic proponents of the old stabilizing-development model had fallen into disrepute. But shared development had failed too, since it had not found the means to ensure the rapid economic growth, foreign exchange, and government income necessary for such a strategy. Yet the wheels for a new strategy had been set in motion during the Echeverría years. The increased investment in the petroleum industry would give birth to a new strategy, one that many state managers saw as a way out, if not a panacea, for Mexico's economic and political woes.

Trump Card: Petroleum for Export

With the failure of shared development, José López Portillo, as the PRI's official candidate for the 1976 presidential election and therefore Mexico's incoming president, put his closest advisers to work in the search for a solution to Mexico's political and economic crisis. In this regard, López Portillo had two political priorities that any strategy chosen must satisfy: the restoration of business confidence, and the establishment of popular confidence in the regime. In fact, López Portillo's 'solution'—rapid petroleum exploitation and exportation—had begun to germinate during the Echeverría years, with increasing investments in petroleum and the growing realization among some PEMEX bureaucrats that exportation on a sizeable scale was feasible. At the same time there was considerable resistance within PEMEX to such an export oriented strategy from the 'Generation of '38,' the engineers, technicians, and managers who went to work for the newly formed government-owned enterprise after the expropriation in that year of the British- and American-dominated oil industry.

To understand the position of these conservationist-technocrats is to understand the historical circumstances surrounding the nationalization of the Mexican petroleum industry and its central importance in Mexican history. Although the immediate events precipitating the oil expropriation related to

[56]

the foreign companies' refusal to implement an arbitrated wage settlement, there were much larger issues at stake during the dispute. As pointed out in the previous chapter, the oil expropriation has a central place in Mexican nationalism and revolutionary mythology. PEMEX's role was expected to be the fulfillment of a vital nationalistic and social function. It was to ensure the supply of national petroleum needs, provide subsidized fuel to the private sector as a stimulus to indigenous industrialization, and provide high wages as well as pay for schools and roads for its workers.

While the 1938 expropriation produced the exit of many trained technocrats, there existed—at the time of the expropriation—a small pool of trained Mexican personnel in the partially government-owned company *Petróleo de Mexico* (Petromex). This company had been set up by the government in 1925 as the National Petroleum Administration, under a new government department in charge of petroleum matters.[30] It was these technocrats who took over the running of the national petroleum industry after the expropriation. As government bureaucrats unconnected with foreign oil interests, their views were nationalistic in outlook. They felt that national petroleum production should be geared largely toward the satisfaction of domestic needs. National interests were to be protected through conservation and through the company's subsidizing the private sector by providing low-cost energy. Even those PEMEX technocrats desirous of making PEMEX more of a business concern than a social organization argued that 'it is illusory . . . to pretend that petroleum produced and exported in large quantities could become the factotum of Mexico's economy or the panacea for Mexico's economic ills.'[31]

The major concern of these technocrats by the late 1960s was the absence of sufficient resources to ensure the enterprise's ability to supply the domestic market. PEMEX by 1968 was calling for the exploitation of hitherto unexplored areas.[32] The pressure of

---

30 Richard B. Manke, *Mexican Oil and Natural Gas* (New York: Praeger, 1979), p. 76.

31 Antonio J. Bermúdez, *The Mexican National Oil Industry* (Stanford, CA: Stanford University Press, 1963), p. 115. Bermúdez was director general of PEMEX from 1948 to 1954.

32 PEMEX, *Programa de operación para 1968* (México, D.F.: PEMEX, 1967), p. 11.

PEMEX technocrats, combined with PEMEX's decreasing capacity to supply the country's petroleum needs and the drain this represented on foreign exchange earnings, was strong enough to produce a mandate for increased investment in the petroleum sector. In 1970 Echeverría launched an $18 billion investment program to locate new petroleum resources and to ensure self-sufficiency.[33]

As capital became more plentiful PEMEX moved into the exploration of new regions, among them the southeast, which would bear fruit in 1972, and the company produced studies outlining the possibilities of reserves off the Gulf along the coasts of Veracruz and Tamaulipas. In 1972 the big discoveries of the Reforma fields in Tabasco and Chiapas occurred. But the old PEMEX technocracy was reluctant to allow the possibilities of Mexico's petroleum potential to become known. This reluctance was both ideological and technical. The technocratic faction—led by its major spokesman Engineer Francisco Inguanzo, manager of exploitation—took the position that not only was the vision of Mexico as a major petroleum exporter undesirable, but that existing technical information failed to support the argument that Mexico was capable of becoming so. This group opposed the newer, riskier method of exploration, which essentially promised increased reserves on the basis of widely dispersed drilling in unknown or partially known basins. This newer method was, however, supported by petroleum technocrats such as César Baptista, head of industrial production. These petroleros saw increased exploitation and exportation as both feasible and desirable for Mexico. It was foolish, they argued, not to take advantage of a natural resource that they believed Mexico had an abundance of.[34] This group became particularly active in pressing for more investment in exploration. They submitted a technical report, suppressed by PEMEX's conservative leadership, that outlined what they believed to be Mexico's substantial petroleum reserves. The conservative conservationist faction apparently believed increased pressure from the United States to step up

---

33 George W. Grayson, *The Politics of Mexican Oil* (Pittsburgh: University of Pittsburgh Press, 1980), p. 47.

34 Members of this faction did not, however, necessarily agree with the rapidity of later exploitation. This will be discussed further in the following chapter.

petroleum production would occur should large reserve figures be made public. In 1973 the director general of PEMEX, Jaime Duvali, publicly stated his opposition to Mexico becoming an exporter of crude.[35] Whether Echeverría was aware of Mexico's petroleum potential has been a subject of some debate. But even if he did know, his nationalist bent would likely have inhibited him from making such information public.[36]

But López Portillo had a different agenda. He was determined to be a popular president, both with the business community and the public in general. Upon taking power in December of 1976 he would be saddled with the unpopular (though not particularly onerous) IMF stabilization program, which limited borrowing and government spending and held down wages. Achieving López Portillo's political priorities called for strong measures: he needed to find a solution to Mexico's foreign exchange dilemma; he needed to restore Mexico's credit worthiness and high growth rates; and he wanted to ensure the adequate flow of resources into government coffers. High growth rates, it was hoped, would provide an adequate supply of jobs. Since López Portillo saw government spending as an essential instrument to restore economic growth and strengthen his political support, rapid petroleum exploitation and exporting appeared to provide the ideal solution.

After having become the PRI's candidate for the 1976 election, López Portillo approached PEMEX officials for details of Mexico's petroleum wealth. He was met with stiff resistance from the PEMEX technocrats, who were unwilling to provide information that would indicate the existence of large reserves. Shortly thereafter, López Portillo drew together a team of experts to study the energy question, appointing his close friend and petroleum contractor Jorge Díaz Serrano as chairman.

Díaz Serrano's role in the Mexican petroleum industry traces its roots to the mid-1950s when, as a contractor for PEMEX, he established the basis for his fortune. Due to business generated by PEMEX, Díaz Serrano was able to create five petroleum con-

---

35 *Proceso*, núm. 118 (5 de Febrero 1979): 40.
36 One argument is that Echeverría was in fact aware of Mexico's petroleum potential but that he wished to leave López Portillo a 'blank check' that would enable him to reestablish legitimacy and confidence.

tracting companies in eight years.[37] Díaz Serrano, himself an oilman and entrepreneur, was able to extract the information regarding Mexico's petroleum potential that the president had so desperately hoped for. With many close contacts built up over the years with PEMEX technocrats, Díaz Serrano gained the cooperation of those PEMEX dissidents who believed that Mexico's petroleum deposits were far greater than was being admitted officially. If petroleum was the lever of future Mexican development, Díaz Serrano's subsequent report to the president outlining Mexico's petroleum potential was the feat that landed him the director-generalship of PEMEX. His report to the president successfully presented data arguing the feasibility of Mexico becoming a major exporter and set up a timetable for its achievement.

Hence, within three weeks of taking power, Díaz Serrano revised Mexico's reserve figures. The official figure for proven reserves of crude petroleum and natural and liquid gas—put at 6.3 billion barrels during the final days of the Echeverría administration—was increased to 11.6 billion barrels; and by the end of 1977 it had been further increased to 16 billion barrels.[38] The report that Díaz Serrano had presented to López Portillo before his appointment as head of PEMEX formed the basis of his Six-Year Plan for the petroleum industry. First unveiled by Díaz Serrano in December 1976 and officially promulgated in March 1977, the plan called for the doubling of crude production and refining capacity in six years and for the tripling of the country's production of basic petrochemicals.[39] The production goal of 2.25 million barrels of crude per day and of 4000 million cubic feet of

---

37 Between 1956 and 1965, Díaz Serrano formed the following companies: Electrificación Industrial S.A.; Servicios Petroleros E.I.S.A.; Perforaciones Marinas del Golfe (Permargo) S.A.; Dragados S.A.; and in 1965, the Golden Lane Drilling Company based in Houston with George Bush as a partner. *Tiempo 80*, núm. 1820 (21 de Marzo 1977): 11.

38 Frank E. Niering, Jr., 'Mexico: A New Force in World Oil,' *The Petroleum Economist* (March 1979): 111.

39 While the six-year petroleum program appears to have been approved by the president in 1976, its details were not widely known by the public until the March 1977 speech of Díaz Serrano. In 1976 the secretary of finance, Moctezuma Cid, disputed Díaz Serrano's claim that the six-year plan for the petroleum industry had been made public. *Proceso*, núm. 52 (31 de Octubre 1977): 9.

gas per day was to be reached by 1982. Noting that internal resources for the investment program would be insufficient, the plan called for borrowing abroad that would 'not surpass the ability of the institution to pay.'[40]

Conclusions

By the mid-1970s the options available to the Mexican state were becoming increasingly limited. Trapped in an economic model of its own creation but no longer to its liking, the primary concern of the political elite was to safeguard the continuity of the political system. Desperate for a program that would restore economic growth and business confidence and assuage popular unrest, incoming President José López Portillo hit upon the possibility of exporting large amounts of petroleum. The strategy was propelled further by the favorable juncture of escalating prices on the international market and the availability of international financing on favorable terms. But the strategy also had its roots in the dissident attitudes of a faction of the PEMEX technocracy; it believed in the presence of large petroleum reserves and—from the late 1960s onwards—pressured for a reversal of the traditional conservationist policy.

---

40 *Tiempo* 70, núm. 1821 (28 de Marzo 1977): 12.

4
PEMEX Expansionism
and the Politics of
Rapid Petroleum Development

Introduction

President López Portillo chose the petroleum export strategy because he became convinced, given international circumstances, that this strategy would stimulate rapid economic growth and fulfill his most important priorities: the restoration of both business confidence and public support. Voices of caution both within and outside of the state, critical of the strategy of rapid petroleum development, went largely unheeded. From the outset the strategy had powerful and convincing supporters, and as it gathered momentum these vested interests became evermore powerful. The most important supporters of rapid petroleum development were the PEMEX technocracy and its director general, Jorge Díaz Serrano.

PEMEX Technocracy: Expansionism and Presidential Support

With Díaz Serrano's appointment as director general of PEMEX, a new team of technocrats espousing an avowedly expansionist export strategy came to power within that organization. Díaz Serrano brought in the so-called 'Tex men,' such as Ignacio de León who was appointed commercial subdirector of PEMEX and Jesús Chavarría García who became subdirector of exploitation; both men were former petroleum contractors. Díaz Serrano also promoted those dissident PEMEX technocrats who supported his

[63]

expansionist strategy. César Baptiste for example was appointed advisor to the director general. The 'generation of '38' either retired or remained within PEMEX, resigned but unhappy with the new strategy.

Díaz Serrano and his new team were the most obvious source of pressure for the new expansionist petroleum program. Firmly believing that petroleum should be exploited and exported as rapidly as possible, they argued that the upswing in the petroleum market was transitory and that the government should therefore take advantage of the situation to acquire as much foreign exchange as possible. Díaz Serrano saw no negative repercussions in such a strategy; in his own words, 'Petroleum is like tomatoes or pineapples. Either they are consumed or lost.'[1]

An important corollary of this policy orientation was the liberal importation of machinery and equipment, since national industry could not supply the inputs that were essential for so rapid an expansion of the petroleum industry. Another implication of the strategy was an ever-growing dependence on private petroleum contractors, including foreign ones, since Mexico lacked the technology and equipment to exploit lucrative offshore reserves. Nor was expansion of the country's refining capacity or of its petrochemical industry—notwithstanding statements to the contrary—of great concern to the proponents of this strategy. The emphasis was on the exploration and extraction of crude since it was felt that Mexico should take advantage of high international prices while they lasted.[2] The strategy also encouraged, if it did not condone, corruption. Although corruption within the Mexican public bureaucracy generally and within PEMEX in particular has been a permanent feature of Mexican political life, there is no question that it accelerated during the petroleum boom, especially within PEMEX. The rapidity with which petroleum development was pursued and the massive

1 *Proceso*, núm. 286 (26 de Abril 1979): 8.
2 A study of PEMEX's investment policies argues that PEMEX slowed down its exploration activity and decreased its expenditure in this area in any given year as soon as a sufficient number of discoveries were made. It did this in order to direct investment toward extraction. Abderrahmane Megateli, *Investment Policies of National Oil Companies* (New York: Praeger, 1980), p. 131. An examination of PEMEX's budget and expenditure pattern during the period shows a marked bias toward exploration and extraction.

inflow of resources that this development brought with it rendered adequate control mechanisms problematic. Indeed, it was believed by PEMEX's top administrators that such mechanisms should probably be avoided as they would slow down the rate of petroleum development.

PEMEX's new administrative team supported a continual revision upward of the petroleum production ceiling. For them, the production goal outlined in the Six-Year Plan of 2.25 million barrels per day by 1982 was not a ceiling but a minimum figure. In March of 1978 PEMEX revised the production goal to reach the level of 2.25 million barrels per day by 1980—or *two years* faster than initially planned. By 1979, Díaz Serrano was lobbying the president for a production level of 4 million barrels per day by 1982.

Between 1977 and 1980, Jorge Díaz Serrano was highly successful in securing the president's full support for his expansionist program. The fact that he was a close friend of the president, and enjoyed direct access to him which could not be matched by any other presidential adviser, undoubtedly gave Díaz Serrano the edge in persuading the president of the efficacy of rapid petroleum development. But more important was the apparent success of the petroleum program in terms of the president's political priorities and Díaz Serrano's growing prestige and influence as he fulfilled the goals of that program. The expansionist strategy did appear to be 'solving' Mexico's political and economic crisis. It was providing capital along with rapid economic growth, thereby making it possible, so it was believed, to restore public confidence in the regime. The fact of Mexico's petroleum wealth made that country extremely attractive for foreign loans. In May 1977, Díaz Serrano brought in the international firm of De Grolyer and McNaughton to satisfy any doubts of the financial and banking worlds about Mexico's claimed reserves; after this review foreign loans were rapidly forthcoming. Henceforth, banks were clamoring to make loans to Mexico. In the words of a senior government official, 'The money seeks us out and at times it has been difficult to choose the best offer.'[3] Because of its petroleum wealth, Mexico was able to abandon the unpopular 1976 IMF agreement in 1978. Due to oil

---

3 Jesús Silva Herzog, subsecretary of finance, in 1980. *Razones*, no. 76 (29 Noviembre–12 Diciembre 1982): 15.

discoveries and consequent foreign borrowing, the IMF loans were paid off in advance. Henceforth López Portillo pursued an expansionary government-expenditure program deemed essential to restore economic growth and public confidence in his regime.

With the president's commitment to a policy that based economic growth on the rapid exploitation and exportation of petroleum and the acquisition of debt, the power of PEMEX and of Díaz Serrano expanded rapidly. The increasing importance of petroleum in the Mexican economy made PEMEX's activities of central importance to economic policymaking. PEMEX's importance in obtaining foreign loans has already been mentioned. The enterprise's share of the public-sector foreign debt went from 11.3 percent in 1976 to 22.6 percent in 1980, and to 29.2 percent by 1981.[4] At the same time PEMEX took an increasing share of the federal government's expenditures until 1980. PEMEX expenditure as a percentage of total government expenditure went from 19.4 percent to 26.6 percent between 1977 and 1980.[5]

Originally the president's economic plan had called for three stages: the first using petroleum dollars to overcome the crisis, a second involving a period of consolidation, while the third stage was to be one of accelerated growth.[6] In fact, this second stage was bypassed. After a brief period of adherence to the IMF stabilization program, the government embarked on an expansionary program of state expenditure and investment. Beginning in 1979 PEMEX became a financial instrument of the state, obtaining loans for other parts of the government.

Another indication of the growing importance of petroleum in the Mexican economy was its importance in the value of exports. Whereas in 1976 petroleum and its derivatives accounted for 16.8 percent of the value of all exports, by 1980 this figure had reached 67.4 percent, and by 1981, 74.4 percent. The federal taxes paid by PEMEX as a percentage of total taxes collected by the federal government went from 5 percent in 1976 to 24.9 percent by 1981, making PEMEX the single-most important taxpayer.[7]

---

4 See Appendix Table 2.5
5 See Appendix Table 3.4
6 José López Portillo, 'Segundo informe presidencial,' *Commercio exterior* 28, no. 9 (Septiembre 1977): 1105.
7 These figures are from Appendix Table 1.2.

With petroleum as the axle of the Mexican economy, Díaz Serrano became for a brief period the most successful of López Portillo's top advisers. The PEMEX chief may even have exaggerated Mexico's reserve figures in order to increase his prestige and stature and that of PEMEX within the political bureaucracy.[8] But even without such tactics, the expansionist strategy was a great 'success.' The production of ever larger quantities of petroleum attested to PEMEX's entrepreneurial capabilities and its director general's administrative success, while the economic growth and revenues generated by petroleum expansion would enable the president to fulfill his political priorities. When PEMEX reached its production goals ahead of time, 1980 instead of 1982, the growing status of Díaz Serrano prompted the rumor that he was a contender to succeed López Portillo. Petroleum policy was made largely by the president and Díaz Serrano with little or no consultation of the Economic Cabinet whose responsibility it supposedly was to direct economic policy.[9] Certain areas, such as the external prices of petroleum, were left to the PEMEX bureaucracy entirely, requiring only presidential approval.[10]

Not surprisingly PEMEX began to tread upon the jurisdictions of other government entities. PEMEX's role in international affairs expanded as its director general traveled to Europe and the United States negotiating credit and trade deals, sometimes accompanied by the secretary of finance. The revision of Article 27 of the Constitution which made petroleum a priority sector and made ejidal and communal lands subject to expropriation for petroleum exploitation, without the usual judicial proceedings,

---

8 Certainly international petroleum circles regarded them with some skepticism. *The Petroleum Times* (December 1, 1978).

9 The precise composition of the Economic Cabinet varies from administration to administration. Under President López Portillo it consisted of the secretaries of natural resources and industrial development, finance, commerce, budget and planning, and labor, the director of the Central Bank, and the chairman of the Office of Economic Advisers to the President (the president's personal advisory team).

10 Until the petroleum-price fiasco of 1981 (discussed in Chapter 7), external prices of petroleum were established by a small group of technocrats in PEMEX who had had many years' experience in the setting of international petroleum prices. Since Díaz Serrano had no expertise in this area, he generally accepted the recommendations of his technocrats and then sought presidential approval.

infringed upon the authority of the secretary of agriculture who had ultimate authority over ejidal lands.

As the expansionist strategy took hold and as PEMEX's power expanded, groups outside and within the state became strong supporters of the perpetuation of the strategy. These groups, many of whom had arisen and been strengthened by rapid petroleum development, represented, as we shall see, important obstacles to any reorientation of policy. Perhaps most obviously, the PEMEX technocracy itself strongly supported the expansionist strategy advocated by Díaz Serrano and his personal team. Díaz Serrano was an extremely popular director general with career professionals. He was highly respected as a petroleum entrepreneur and as a director general who could 'get things done.' Although the PEMEX technocracy may have had some reservations about specific aspects of Díaz Serrano's strategy, most were very much in agreement with the general thrust of his program.[11] Rapid petroleum development expanded the power, prestige, and budget of PEMEX, and therefore expanded career opportunities. Lower-level officials were not adverse to publicly expressing their support for Díaz Serrano's expansionary program.[12] And PEMEX technocrats, preoccupied with their own career advancement, pursued Díaz Serrano's goal of ever-larger quantities of petroleum production with unbounded enthusiasm.[13]

---

11 Lower-level PEMEX technocrats took a dim view of the use of PEMEX to 'subsidize the rest of the economy' through low domestic oil and gas prices and through the use of PEMEX to obtain loans for other state entities. Some expressed concern about the rapidity of production and about the loss of administrative control that this entailed. Career interests and the hierarchical nature of the authority structure, however, generally inhibited the articulation of such reservations.

12 The subdirector of Economic Studies and Planning of PEMEX, along with the subdirector of the Instituto Mexicano de Petróleo, called for the abolition of any sort of petroleum production ceiling. *Unomásuno* (16 de Mayo 1980): 1.

13 Those who have examined the internal workings of the Mexican bureaucracy argue that bureaucrats, concerned with career advancement, pursue the goals and priorities of their superiors, who in turn pursue policies that will enhance the power and prestige of those to whom they are responsible, on up to the president. Central to all of this is the avoidance of risky policies, which would be harmful to the career interests of one's superiors and therefore to oneself. See for example Guy Benveniste, *Bureaucracy and National Planning: A Sociological Case Study in Mexico* (New York: Praeger, 1977). As in all bureaucracies,

PEMEX expansionism was also pushed relentlessly forward by its almost continuous success in discovering new reserves. A new oil field was discovered in Chicontepec in late 1978 while exploration in the Bay of Campeche pushed production of these offshore reserves to one-third of total production by 1980. Between 1978 and 1979 Mexico doubled its estimates of the country's proven reserves from 20 billion barrels to 40 billion. By 1980, the figure was 50 billion.[14] For many PEMEX technocrats the petroleum production ceiling had to be increased simply because it could be. The bureaucratic goals of career advancement and institutional expansion were of paramount importance to PEMEX officials, who as a consequence pushed petroleum exploitation relentlessly forward.

PEMEX's Allies and Fellow Travelers

Within the public bureaucracy there were other departments and agencies that shared PEMEX's enthusiasm for the rapid exploitation of petroleum. These departments and agencies also became important sources of pressure for the continuation of that program. These were the so-called 'political' departments and agencies whose various public clienteles had to be satisfied with rapidly expanding government spending. C. Hank González, head of the Federal District, was one of Díaz Serrano's strongest supporters and highly committed to an expansionary spending program. While the budget of the Federal District increased rapidly during the period, González firmly resisted any increase in taxes or prices.[15] González was himself closely linked to the petroleum industry. Although beginning humbly as a school teacher and later as a bureaucrat for the State of Mexico's Department of Secondary Education, he was able to amass a considerable for-

---

larger questions—such as whether a policy is in the long-term interests of the country as a whole (however that may be defined)—get lost in the shuffle of bureaucratic self-interest and 'empire building.'

14 *The Petroleum Economist* (January 1979): 39; ibid., April 1980, p. 175.

15 *Proceso*, núm. 214 (8 de Diciembre 1980): 22. Most of the Federal District's budget goes to public transportation, including the subway, along with other metropolitan services.

tune, eventually getting into the business of supplying pipe to PEMEX through his steel complex of Campos Hermanos.[16] González had supporters throughout the bureaucracy and the PRI and was a key supporter of President López Portillo. Other government agencies such as CONASUPO and the Electrical Commission (CFE) also supported an expansionary program as it made available to them plentiful resources that could provide the patronage necessary to satisfy clients. Especially in the case of agencies providing services and goods to the public, insufficient resources make the task of keeping the lid on social unrest that much more difficult.

The strongest union in the country—the Union of Oil Workers of the Mexican Republic (STPRM)—was another source of pressure for Díaz Serrano's expansionist program. In 1975 certain older leaders of the union, those who had participated in the nationalization of the oil industry and were opposed to oil exports, were replaced by a younger group who supported the expansionist export program. Traditionally the oil union has been very supportive of the PRI and has had close ties with the top levels of the public bureaucracy and political elite, especially with the secretary of labor and the president. It has played a centrally important role, given its predominance as a local political force, in linking local loyalties through the union to the PRI and the federal government.[17] The union exchanges its political support for economic benefits: it is a major subcontractor for PEMEX, having since the 1950s been granted 50 percent of the industry's contracts.[18] The union also receives from the contracting companies 5 percent of the salary of the workers employed by them.[19] Relations between the oil union and the administration of President López Portillo were particularly close. It is well known that 'La Quina' (nickname of the powerful chief of the union's Madero City local, Joaquín Hernández Galicia) had easy

16 *Razones*, núm. 27 (12–25 de Enero 1981): 9.
17 Marie-France Prevot-Shapira, 'Trabajadores del petróleo y poder sindical en México,' in Miguel S. Wionczek, coord., *Energía en México: Ensayos sobre el pasado y presente* (México, D.F.: El Colegio de México, 1982), p. 162.
18 Jerry R. Ladman et al., eds., *U.S.–Mexican Energy Relationships* (Toronto: D. C. Heath, 1981), p. 55.
19 Lourdes Orozco, 'PEMEX y la crises del petróleo,' *Cuadernos politicos*, núm. 15 (Enero–Marzo 1978): 88.

access to the president. The alliance between the oil union and the state was further cemented under the directorship of Díaz Serrano, who agreed that 2 to 2.5 percent of every contract let to an outside firm would be contributed to the union's social fund.[20] PEMEX has also obliged the union by helping it to suppress dissident elements within the ranks through transferring activists who are troublesome.

The rapid expansion of the petroleum industry enriched the oil workers union tremendously. Hence, it was able to provide ample benefits to its workers in the form of high wages, credit, housing, and medical care, thereby ensuring their acquiescence (if not loyalty) while making possible the enrichment of union leaders. Corruption increased during the period of the petroleum boom with an explosion in the selling of jobs and the embezzlement of union funds.

The private business sector that dealt directly with PEMEX was also strongly supportive of the rapid exploitation and exportation of petroleum. Indeed, those entrepreneurs supplying the petroleum industry, the petroleum labor leaders, and top PEMEX technocrats have been tightly intertwined in a mutuality of interests that in Mexico is known as a *camarilla*.[21] Although the central place of PEMEX in the Mexican revolutionary mythology might suggest a role as defender of popular national interests, in fact this has been less and less the case in recent years. Since its establishment PEMEX has been a source of enrichment for politicians and entrepreneurs. Even politicians who had participated in the Revolution quite often set up trucking firms serving PEMEX and the petrochemical industry.[22] Starting in the 1950s, PEMEX's top administration began to establish close links with private-sector contracting companies. Antonio Bermúdez, director general from 1948 to 1958, was particularly supportive of using private contracting companies.

---

20 George W. Grayson, *The Politics of Mexican Oil* (Pittsburgh: University of Pittsburgh Press, 1980), p. 100; Fen Hampson and Kevin Middlebrook, 'Energy Security in North America,' in David A. Deese and Joseph S. Nye, eds., *Energy and Security* (Cambridge, MA: Ballinger, 1981), p. 167.

21 Alliances between state managers and their clients outside the state for financial rewards.

22 Edward J. Williams, *The Rebirth of the Mexican Petroleum Industry* (Toronto: D. C. Heath, 1979), p. 113.

It was during the late 1940s and 1950s that the PEMEX camarilla arose. PEMEX superintendent Jaime Merino de la Peña was appointed in 1942 to oversee the exploitation of what was then the richest petroleum area in Mexico, Poza Rica. He became a multimillionaire providing lucrative contracts to such favored private contractors as Jorge Díaz Serrano. During this same period, the notorious petroleum labor leader Pedro Vivanco violently subdued any popular unrest, especially those petroleum workers who protested the camarilla's corrupt practices.[23] The lucrative practice whereby labor leaders and top PEMEX technocrats held positions on the boards of directors of private petroleum-contracting companies had originated during these years.

While the role of the private sector in the Mexican oil industry remained marginal up until 1970, President López Portillo's project of rapid petroleum development gave impetus to the role of the private sector, especially that of foreign contracting companies. The desire to find oil reserves quickly meant that by October of 1977 PEMEX had already signed ten outside contracts to supplement its drilling capacity.[24] Offshore production created a pressing need for foreign technology. In 1977 PEMEX hired the American firm Brown and Root for an estimated $500 million to organize facilities for future offshore production from the Bay of Campeche.[25] Mexican and foreign firms were contracted to do pipelaying, onshore and offshore construction, and various engineering operations.[26] PEMEX also established links with foreign firms through licensing arrangements. The first Mexican-made oil rig, for example, was built under license from Dresser Industries Incorporated of Houston.[27] In addition a massive amount of machinery and equipment for the petroleum industry was purchased from foreign, especially U.S., firms. In 1981 alone, American oil equipment companies sold $2 billion worth of equipment to PEMEX.[28] Contracting and licenses were also

---

23 For a discussion of this period, see *Proceso*, no. 110 (11 de Diciembre 1978): 14.
24 Fen Osler Hampson, *Fraught with Risk: The Political Economy of Petroleum Policies in Canada and Mexico* (Ph.D. diss., Harvard University, 1982), p. 324.
25 *The Petroleum Economist* (September 1977): 374.
26 See *The Petroleum Economist* and *The Petroleum Times* between 1977 and 1981.
27 *The Petroleum Times* (July 23, 1976): 9.
28 *New York Times* (May 13, 1982): D7.

extremely important in the basic petrochemical industry, which the state monopolized. Foreign companies were encouraged to enter downstream in the manufacture of secondary petrochemicals with the result that foreign companies established subsidiaries to supply services and equipment to PEMEX.

The most powerful Mexican business interests benefited enormously from the petroleum exportation program, especially that faction of the business sector which had been so hostile to the Echeverría administration—the Monterrey group. The Monterrey group is also the Mexican business sector most closely tied to multinational capital, through licenses, patents, and the direct investment of foreign firms in Mexican firms.[29] It also depends heavily for credit on American banks, especially for the purchase of foreign technology. HYSLA, of the ALFA subgroup of Monterrey, Mexico's main private producer of steel, was one of the enterprises most stimulated by the petroleum boom. Indeed, ALFA expanded extremely rapidly during the period, moving into such industries as petrochemicals. The subgroup CYDSA, Mexico's second-largest producer of chemicals, also benefited enormously from the expansionist strategy.

It was domestic and foreign enterprises closely connected with the petroleum industry that gained the most from the government's expansionist strategy and became its strongest supporters. Patronage schemes—such as Díaz Serrano's 'Plan Chicontepec', which would have provided lucrative contracts to the end of the century—bound these private-sector interests and the PEMEX technocracy tightly together in mutual self-interest.

Much was said during the period about alleged U.S. pressure on Mexico to produce ever larger quantities of petroleum. There is no question that the United States became extremely interested in Mexico as an alternative and stable source of energy following the 1973 world oil crisis and Arab oil embargo.[30] Indeed, a report

---

29 Conexiones y Tubería, S.A., of the subgroup CYDSA is associated with B. F. Goodrich Chemical Co. In 1975, the ALFA group joined with the American company Dupont to purchase two Mexican synthetic fiber companies, participating with 40 percent of the shares. ALFA also has ties with Union Carbide and International Nickle of Canada. *Proceso*, núm. 78 (1 de Mayo 1978): 17–18.
30 Mexico was seen as offering 'the United States and its allies significant oppor-

prepared by the Senate Committee on Energy and Natural Resources recommended that the United States encourage Mexico to develop a permanent overcapacity for petroleum production that could be utilized rapidly and that would permit the exportation of extra Mexican crude in the case of an 'international energy emergency.'[31] Despite American interest in increased Mexican oil production, however, official pronouncements showed considerable restraint, perhaps influenced by advice that a more aggressive policy would arouse Mexican nationalist sensibilities and that too rapid development could have a destabilizing influence.[32] More important than pressure exerted from north of the border in determining the momentum of the petroleum export strategy, was the pressure exerted by PEMEX technocrats and their private-sector allies, both domestic and foreign. But the strategy, as the following section will show, did not solve Mexico's economic problems and in many ways deepened them, thereby generating growing political tensions.

Economic Implications of Rapid Petroleum Development

The petroleum export strategy did fulfill one of López Portillo's most important economic goals. Economic growth was restored with annual growth rates averaging 8.5 percent per year for 1978–1981.[33] However, aspects of Mexico's economic disequilibrium not only failed to disappear but were apparently exaggerated by the petroleum–debt strategy itself. As Mexico's appetite for imports increased, her balance of trade remained in a deficit position from 1974. After having achieved some improvement during the early years of the López Portillo administration, the relationship of the deficit of the current account to gross domestic

---

tunities for reducing their dependence upon Middle East Oil.' *Hearings before the Committee on Energy and Natural Resources: 2nd Session on the Geopolitics of Oil* (Washington, DC: Government Printing Office, 1980), p. 225.

31 U.S. Senate, *Geopolitics of Oil: Hearings before the Committee on Energy and Natural Resources* (Washington, DC: Government Printing Office, 1980), p. 309.

32 Statement of Dr. David Ronfeldt, energy consultant, Rand Corporation, *Geopolitics of Oil: Hearings before the Committee on Energy and Natural Resources* (Washington, DC: Government Printing Office, 1980), p. 289 ff.

33 See Appendix Table 1.1.

product reached 3.5 percent in 1979 and a record 4.9 percent in 1981.[34]

A number of factors connected to rapid petroleum development seem to have contributed to this phenomenon. It would appear that the initial effort to get the petroleum flowing required import- and capital-investment outlays greater than export receipts. PEMEX's participation in total imports of the public sector went from 18.5 percent in 1970 to 44.8 percent by 1980.[35]

Other disturbing indicators included stagnation in manufacturing exports. Beginning in 1978 manufactured products began to lose their share of the value of total exports.[36] Even more pressing was the agricultural crisis. Starting from a situation of self-sufficiency in agriculture in the mid-1960s, by 1980 one-quarter of all foodstuffs had to be imported.[37] While agriculture as well lost its share of the value of total exports, the value of food exports also declined in absolute terms from 1979 to 1981. Food production for domestic consumption failed to keep pace with population growth, with the result that while food represented 4 percent of the value of total imports in 1976, by 1982 the figure was 13.1 percent.[38] The inflow of capital brought about by rapid petroleum development produced an overvalued currency that, largely for reasons of national pride, was not devalued. This overvaluation of local currency rendered nonpetroleum exports increasingly less competitive. In the agricultural sector, climactic factors intensified the problems already deepened by policy neglect and by a single-minded emphasis on rapid petroleum development. Mexico, it would appear, had succumbed to one of the most common political pressures of petrolization: that of taking the easy way out by using petroleum wealth to purchase food and manufactured inputs. The shortfall between foreign exchange earnings and requirements was made up by foreign borrowing.

34 Gabriel Székely, *La economía política del petróleo en México, 1976–1982* (México, D.F.: El Colegio de México, 1983): 128–129, Table 20.

35 Alejandro Carrillo Castro and Sergio Garcí Ramírez, *Las empresas públicas en México* (México, D.F.: Miguel Angel Porrúa, 1983), p. 155.

36 Manufacturing exports fell from 42 percent of the value of total exports in 1978 to 19.3 percent by 1980. See Appendix Table 1.2.

37 Gustavo Esteva, *The Struggle for Rural Mexico* (South Hadley, MA: Bergin and Garvey, 1983), p. 9.

38 See Appendix Table 1.2

The expansionist strategy did not provide for a generalized improvement in living standards. Although employment grew at the average annual rate of 4.7 percent between 1979 and 1981, its expansion occurred largely in construction and public works, areas that are not long-term job producers.[39] The petroleum sector, given its capital-intensive nature, was not an important job producer. Between 1973 and 1980 employment in the petroleum sector increased only 5 percent.[40] The socioeconomic situation of the popular classes, especially the rural poor, most probably worsened during the period. As the inflow of capital stimulated inflation the purchasing power of the population declined. One study shows that minimum real salaries fell by an accumulated index of 12 percent between 1977 and 1980, before increasing a small amount in 1981.[41] With the crisis in the agrarian sector, rural–urban migration continued unabated and the numbers of underemployed in the urban sector increased.

While this situation began to worry policymakers, generating an intense intrabureaucratic struggle (the subject of Chapter 5), it was also arousing increasing social and political unrest. By 1980 the petroleum expansionist strategy had pitted its beneficiaries against those who were losing because of it.

Opposition to the Petroleum Expansionist Strategy

President López Portillo, concerned about the popularity of his administration, had sought to incorporate dissident groups through liberalizing the political process. The president's Federal Law of Electoral Political Organization, enacted in 1977, widened participation for opposition parties while his 1979 Amnesty Law

---

39 Gabriel Székely, *La economía política del petróleo en México, 1976–1982*, p. 109.

40 Socrates C. Rizzo, 'Generation and Allocation of Oil Economic Surpluses,' in Pedro Aspe and Paul E. Sigmund, eds., *The Political Economy of Income Distribution in Mexico* (New York: Holmes and Meier, 1984), p. 118.

41 Gabriel Székely, *La economía política del petróleo en México, 1976–1982*, p. 134. In fact these figures underestimate the negative impact on living standards as minimum wage figures exclude the large proportion of the population (40 to 50 percent) that are underemployed and receive less than the minimum wage and no social benefits.

was also designed to assuage opposition groups.[42] Yet his economic policies intensely alienated precisely those groups that his political program was designed to incorporate. Moreover the broadened participation afforded opposition parties gave the regime's opponents a public forum where they could air their views.

The most vociferous opposition to the petroleum expansionist's strategy came from the leftist parties and dissidents, who articulated the growing discontent of disadvantaged groups. Opposition was particularly violent from peasants in the petroleum-producing areas. The governors and traditional elites of these regions were also distressed at the social and economic dislocation caused by rapid petroleum development. Opposition came as well from certain worker and professional organizations, from the academic community, and even from within the PRI, particularly from local Party members in the petroleum-producing states.

There were a number of specific issues that galvanized these opposition groups. Of particular importance to peasants was a bill sent to Congress in December 1977 proposing an amendment to Article 27 of the Constitution; it stipulated that all lands were to be made subject to immediate expropriation if oil and gas deposits were discovered. This gave PEMEX and petroleum exploitation priority over all other surface or subsoil rights, including ejidal and communal tenancies. The government was caused considerable embarrassment when a congressman from the campesino section of the PRI, Victor Manzanilla Schaffer, spoke out against the bill, denouncing it as unconstitutional and contrary to the spirit of the Mexican Revolution's agrarian reform. Manzanilla Schaffer's support for the opposition in voting against the bill precipitated demands for his resignation, but the controversy eventually died down and he remained in Congress. It was only on condition that PEMEX make appropriate compen-

---

42 According to the new electoral legislation, a party could achieve official registration if it received 1.5 percent of the vote or demonstrated a membership of 65,000. One-quarter of the House of Deputies was now to be elected by proportional representation. For a critique of López Portillo's political reform, see Cecilia Imaz, 'La izquierda y la reforma política en México: Situación actual y perspectivas de la democracia,' *Revista mexicana de sociología* 42, núm. 3 (Julio–Septiembre 1981).

sation payments to peasants whose lands had been expropriated—or were about to be—that the peasant section of the PRI supported the constitutional amendment in Congress. Local leaders of the CNC (the National Peasant Confederation) in Veracruz and Chiapas spoke out against the proposed bill demanding land rather than compensation because, in their words, 'we are not going to eat petroleum.'[43]

The issue was an important one as it hit hard at one of the myths of the Mexican revolutionary ideology, that the government was the defender of peasant property rights and the custodian of agrarian reform. Moreover this legislation—combined with the lack of adequate and timely compensation for expropriated and contaminated land—produced rising unrest among peasants in the petroleum zones. From 1975 onward peasant unrest grew, particularly in the state of Tabasco, Mexico's newest petroleum center, which was receiving massive amounts of investment for petroleum exploitation. In 1976, 7000 campesinos from four Tabasco municipalities united to become the Pacto Ribereno; throughout the period this campesino league battled PEMEX for compensation. In order to press their demands, campesinos of the Pact blocked the entry and exit of personnel and vehicles to and from PEMEX installations on a number of occasions. The government's response in the face of this rising agitation was the usual formula of cooptation and repression. The Pact was declared illegal, it was divided through the granting of the demands of some campesinos and not others, it was intimidated by the moving in of army troops, and its leadership was coopted and divided.[44] The issue was supposedly resolved in March of 1979 with an agreement between the state of Tabasco and PEMEX providing for the establishment of a commission to deal with the question of compensation to farmers. The masses of poorer peasants however were not compensated, and the violence continued throughout the sexenio.[45]

---

43 *Unomásuno* (28 de Diciembre 1977): 5.

44 On this see María Guadalupe Velazquez Guzmán, 'Afectaciones petroleras en Tabasco: El movimiento del Pacta Ribereño,' *Revista mexicana de sociología*, núm. 1 (Enero–Marzo 1982).

45 For a chronology of the events in the PEMEX–Tabasco conflict, see *Proceso*, núm. 140 (9 de Julio 1979): 10 ff.

Indeed, between January 1977 and June 1978 forty-two blockades by peasants caused heavy losses to PEMEX.[46] After 1978, with the failure of an agreement between PEMEX and the CNC to solve outstanding issues, peasant blockades of PEMEX installations escalated and were increasingly reported in the press. By February of 1979, Chontal Indian peasants occupied six oil wells and blocked off fifty-five roads to oil fields near Villahermosa, among the most important deposits in the country. The issue was compensation for damaged and expropriated lands.[47] As the tension escalated, PEMEX requested the intervention of government troops to dislodge the campesinos, charging that the remuneration they were demanding was excessive. The peasants were finally dislodged through use of the army. Although official peasant representatives did not speak out in favor of such peasant action, their sympathies were clearly not with PEMEX. National CNC leaders denounced the failure to compensate peasants quickly and fairly and called upon the government to put more resources into rural employment.[48]

But while peasant opposition from the petroleum areas may have been the most violent, it was part of the growing regional opposition to PEMEX's activities. Clearly, rapid petroleum development was having a negative impact on the social and economic conditions of petroleum-producing areas. A rapid rise in cost of living has characterized the petroleum zones, further impoverishing peasants who may already have had their land contaminated or expropriated. There seems to be little question that rapid petroleum exploitation has hastened and deepened the agricultural crisis in the petroleum regions.[49] High migration to these regions due to petroleum activity and the attraction of petroleum wealth have meant inadequate housing, schools, and roads, as population has burgeoned beyond the ability to provide

---

46 Marie-France Prevot-Schapira, 'Trabajadores del petróleo y poder sindical en méxico,' in Miguel S. Wionczek, coord., *Energía en México: Ensayos sobre el pasado y el presente*, p. 166.

47 *Unomásuno* (8 de Febrero 1979): 8.

48 Ibid., 20 de Febrero 1979, p. 1.

49 On Tabasco, see Leopoldo Allub and Marco A. Michel, 'Industria petrolera y cambio regional: El caso de Tabasco,' *Cuadernos del centro de investigación para la integración social* (Marzo 1980).

social amenities.[50] Even in older petroleum zones, such as Poza Rica, social conditions have remained deplorable, with inadequate water supply and sewage disposal. Particularly in the newest petroleum regions, rapid petroleum development has not benefited the local populations. The rural population displaced from its land has been forced to migrate since it is unable to find employment in the closed-shop, skill-intensive petroleum industry. Indeed natives of the State of Tabasco, when they are absorbed into the petroleum industry, occupy the lowest and most unstable positions.[51] The best and most highly paid jobs have been taken by outsiders. Crowding and the lack of social services have produced a growing crime rate, prostitution, and delinquency.

Governors and other state leaders articulated the growing discontent. In Tabasco an alliance between traditional elites and discontented peasants was led by the governor of that state, Leandro Rovirosa Wade, who chastised the federal government for its failure to take measures to alleviate the social conditions created by rapid petroleum development. The growing dissatisfaction of local political leaders more and more revolved around the question of the inadequacy of government resources to meet the social and economic problems created by rapid petroleum development.[52]

Heberto Castillo, leader of the Mexican Worker's Party (PMT) and writer for the weekly magazine *Proceso*, led the leftist political opposition to the government's economic program. Many of his criticisms were echoed by the academic community, although in a less strident fashion. By 1979 all opposition parties were vociferously opposed to the rapidity with which petroleum was being exploited. Conservationists led by Castillo disputed the government's reserve figures. Castillo argued that proven, probable, and potential reserves would be exhausted by the years 1992, 1998, and 2018 respectively,[53] and that by 1997 Mexico would have

---

50 Villahermosa, the capital of Tabasco, went from a population of 99,000 in 1970 to 250,000 by 1979. George W. Grayson, *The Politics of Mexican Oil*, p. 78.

51 See Leopoldo Allub and Marco A. Michel, 'Migración y estructura ocupacional en una región petrolera,' *Revista mexicana de sociología* 42, núm. 1 (Enero–Marzo 1982).

52 Tabasco, for example, producer of 60 percent of Mexico's petroleum during this period, received 9 percent of the taxes that the energy generated.

53 *Proceso*, núm. 73 (27 de Marzo 1978): 31.

to import. Critics were also concerned about the rational use of the petroleum dollars and of the country's capacity to absorb them. It was felt that a policy of rapid petroleum exploitation served American interests in supplying U.S. energy needs and would convert Mexico into a monoexporter of petroleum, rendering it extremely vulnerable to fluctuations in petroleum prices. Nationalists rallied against the increasing use of multinationals, seeing this practice as a direct violation of the Constitution. In addition a great deal of concern was expressed about what appeared to be the growing power and corruption of PEMEX.

Sympathy was expressed for the peasants' plight, and demands were made for an increase in resources in the agricultural sector. Generally, it was argued that the strategy had benefited select groups such as PEMEX employees while leaving out the masses of urban and rural poor, and exacerbating the misery in petroleum areas. The academic community echoed many of these criticisms in the press and in other forums, such as academic conferences to which government officials were invited.[54]

All this criticism produced a certain amount of concern in government circles, as evidenced by the government's efforts to respond to them. Each time Heberto Castillo disputed government figures, a flurry of activity occurred within the Ministry of Natural Resources and Industrial Development as government officials attempted to dispute Castillo's figures. In other cases, the government was simply embarrassed by its inability to counter the opposition's charges with any reasonable explanation. In the face of mounting criticism of PEMEX's burning of gas associated with the production of petroleum, for example, Díaz Serrano 'reduced' the figure of gas burned and announced that the rest had been 'made use of.' Such embarrassments did little for the regime's popular support.

Two issues—controversy over the sale of gas to the United States which raged through 1977 and 1978, and the Ixtoc 1 explosion that occurred in June 1979—gave leftist critics plenty of fuel with which to flame rising nationalist sentiment. Given the large

---

54 For a summary of views expressed at the Colegio de México Conference— 'Petróleo y gas: Problemas y "perspectivas,"' see *Proceso*, núm. 85 (3 de Julio, 1978) and núm. 89 (17 de Julio 1978).

amount of gas produced with Mexican oil in the new petroleum regions of Chiapas and Tabasco, exportation to the United States appeared to be a logical course of action, particularly in the eyes of PEMEX's export-oriented director general, Jorge Díaz Serrano. But from the day the project was announced in June of 1977 the government was put on the defensive by rising criticism from the leftist press and opposition political parties.[55] Critics, led by Heberto Castillo, argued that the project would produce greater economic dependence on the United States.[56] There was also strong nationalist resistance to any reduction in the price already agreed upon between Mexico and the American gas companies, but which the U.S. Congress rejected. Upon the U.S. Congress' rejection, the Mexican government announced that the pipeline would be built to transport gas for purely national purposes. Although the deal eventually went through in September 1979, the maneuverability of the Mexican government was becoming increasingly limited. Both Díaz Serrano and López Portillo had been forced to grant interviews with Heberto Castillo back in early 1977, in order to address some of his concerns. In October of 1977 PEMEX felt compelled to hold two television programs in order to 'explain' the government's position on the 'gasoduct.' And although the government did continue to build the pipeline toward the Texas border, it was forced to drop any further public discussion of the possibility of the sale of gas to the United States. Indeed, it denied that gas would be sold to its northern neighbor even as public officials worked quietly behind the scenes to achieve the 1979 agreement with the United States.[57]

---

55 Good discussions of the 'gasoduct' controversy include Jesús Puente Leyva, 'The Natural Gas Controversy,' in Susan Kaufman Purcell, ed., *Mexico–U.S. Relations* (New York: Praeger, 1981); Richard R. Fagen and Henry R. Nau, 'Mexican Gas: The Northern Connection,' in Richard R. Fagen, ed., *Capitalism and the State in U.S.–Latin American Relations* (Stanford, CA: Stanford University Press, 1981); Henry R. Nau, 'U.S.–Mexican Oil and Gas Relations: A Special Relationship, in Richard E. Erb and Stanley R. Ross, eds., *United States Relations with Mexico: Context and Content* (Washington, DC: American Enterprise Institute for Public Policy Research, 1981).

56 The alternative proposed was to liquify the gas and ship it by tanker to other countries. The government responded that it was far too expensive to do this.

57 The agreement did not bring Mexico what it had wanted. The gas deal agreed to a price of (U.S.) $3.625 per 1000 cubic feet. Mexico had been asking that the price be tied to that of No. 2 fuel, which at that time was $5.00.

The other event that precipitated rising criticism of government policy was the blowout of the Ixtoc 1 offshore well in the Bay of Campeche, which spewed forth oil causing massive ecological damage for almost nine months from June 1979 through March 1980.[58] Critics argued that it was the government's wholesale aim of getting the petroleum out as rapidly as possible that caused it to be careless of safety and ecological precautions. Specific criticisms of the performance of PEMEX and its petroleum contractors included the use of inexperienced and unqualified personnel, inadequate supervisory personnel, and the low priority given to security and to environmentally sound procedures and equipment, due to the desire to cut corners.

Again, the opposition stressed the antinationalism of PEMEX's activities and policies. PEMEX, it was charged, had been converted into a 'U.S. enterprise.'[59] According to Heberto Castillo the drilling company Permargo—which Díaz Serrano set up but had supposedly divested himself of—had in violation of the Mexican Constitution subcontracted the drilling to an American-owned company (Sedco International).[60] The press demanded that Díaz Serrano prove that he had no interest in the private companies involved in the explosion. Opposition critics alleged that the government's subsequent investigation, carried out by *La Procuraduría General de la República*, was a coverup.[61] The issue was further inflamed when it became known in an interview published in a German newspaper that Red Adair, who had been called in to cap the leak, held PEMEX responsible for the disaster.[62]

It was following an intense campaign of the leftist parties that Díaz Serrano was forced to submit in September 1979 to eight hours of questioning before the Chamber of Deputies on PEMEX's performance. Díaz Serrano's testimony was viewed as far from satisfactory and hence did little to sooth rising criticism:

---

58 For a good account, see George W. Grayson, *The Politics of Mexican Oil*, Chapter 9.
59 Ibid., p. 165.
60 The Mexican Constitution prohibits the granting of contracts to foreign enterprises to drill for petroleum (Article 16).
61 Heberto Castillo and Rogelio Narango, *Cuando el petróleo se acaba* (México, D.F.: Ediciones Océano, S.A., 1984), pp. 164, 170.
62 *Proceso*, núm. 171 (22 de Febrero 1980): 18.

the use of foreign companies was justified as being 'necessary,' the contamination caused by the explosion was 'not serious,' according to Díaz Serrano and PEMEX's director general could not explain serious discrepancies in production figures.

Given the emotional nature of the issues involved, protest movements and demonstrations quickly began to unite the various opposition groups. In early 1978 a number of leftist political parties, labor organizations, and academic groups organized a march to protest 'the irrational exploitation of Mexico's resources.' In February of 1979 another march took place; in it participants of the earlier march joined the telephone workers union, the nuclear workers, leaders of dissident sections of the petroleum workers union (Sections 34 and 35), and representatives from the Congreso de Trabajo. This march was in protest against President Carter's visit to Mexico to press for the gas deal between the two countries. In early March 1980, representatives of thirty organizations gathered to reactivate the Front for the Defense of Natural Resources formed in 1978; this coalition supported a limit on petroleum production, an end to low domestic prices for petroleum and gas, a limit on the burning of associated gas, and an end to the use of foreign contracting companies in the petroleum industry for the exploration of hydrocarbons. In March of 1978 the Front staged a demonstration in support of its goals.[63]

Despite the petroleum boom and President López Portillo's 'political reform,' the political tranquility so desperately sought eluded the regime. Labor unrest continued and was sporadically repressed. Strikes had occurred among medical doctors, telephone workers, copper workers, textile workers, and among Mexico-based Volkswagen workers. A major challenge came from the university workers union (SUNTU), who had sought to create a national union. The police and army had been used to bring the striking telephone workers back to work and to dislodge striking copper workers from La Caridad Copper Mill. In early 1978 a new confederation of seventy independent unions had been created.[64] In the rural sector, land invasions and peasant unrest continued.

---

63 Accounts of these events may be found in *Proceso*, núm. 70 (6 de Marzo 1978): 24; núm. 72 (20 de Marzo 1978): 25; núm. 174 (3 de Marzo 1980): 33; and in *Unomásuno* (8 de Febrero 1979): 1.

64 *Latin American Economic Report* (February 10, 1978): 5.

Absenteeism in local and state elections suggested increasing popular alienation from the regime. In short, by 1980 it was by no means certain that the petroleum expansionist strategy had solved Mexico's economic and political problems. And in many ways it had made them worse.

Conclusions

The impetus for the new petroleum export strategy came from the director general of PEMEX and his new administrative team. The director general had succeeded in convincing President López Portillo that the strategy would satisfy his most pressing political priorities: business confidence and popular support. The strategy had strong supporters from within the PEMEX technocracy, which saw its bureaucratic and career interests enormously expanded by the new petroleum export policy. Moreover, these bureaucratic interests were strongly reinforced by PEMEX's tightly knit private-sector ties. Strong support also came from the Petroleum Workers Union and from other parts of the public bureaucracy that looked forward to handsome financial rewards and the ability to readily satisfy clienteles. In addition, once the strategy got under way it generated its own momentum as the power of these vested interests expanded. The change in Mexico's economy brought about by the petroleum export strategy was reflected in an alteration in the power structure of the state. The growing importance of petroleum in Mexico's economy meant that the PEMEX technocracy—and especially its director general, Jorge Díaz Serrano—became predominant in economic policymaking. This predominance, given PEMEX's narrow interests, represented a threat to the unity and coherence of the state. Given the power of PEMEX and of the vested interests tied to the expansionist strategy, it would now be very difficult for state managers to readjust the chosen path once they fully recognized its negative repercussions.

An alliance had been forged between the private sector (domestic and foreign) and those PEMEX technocrats favorable to exportation. The petroleum export strategy benefited Mexico's most powerful industrial financial groups, their multinational allies, along with selected groups among wage labor in activities related to the petroleum industry. It was not so much Díaz Serrano's personal ties to foreign contracting companies but the petroleum strategy itself, and its requirements, that predisposed the state enterprise to a tight mutuality of interests with the private sector. The strategy marginalized the rural and urban poor, but it especially hurt those rural poor displaced by oil production in the newest petroleum-producing regions. The social implications of the strategy combined with its seemingly antinationalist nature evoked strong nationalist and leftist criticism.

The strategy was successful only in the very short term: it facilitated the inflow of capital into government coffers, allowing the president to lubricate the patronage system and thereby shore up political stability. It brought with it fast economic growth rates, creating some jobs in the petroleum and construction industries and helping restore confidence in the regime. The strategy however did not solve—and indeed may have deepened—many of Mexico's most serious problems: severe social and ecological problems existed in the petroleum zones; food and manufacturing production were stagnating; the balance of payments disequilibrium continued; and inflation was increasing. Furthermore, these economic problems were being acted out at the political level in a way that was increasingly threatening the regime's claim to be defender of the nation's resources and of the interests of the popular classes. Like other petroleum export economies, rapid petroleum development had strengthened the state in only a superficial sense. While the inflow of capital into government coffers made it easier to look after clienteles, the process of rapid petroleum development was generating social unrest that was eroding popular support.

As we shall see in the following chapter, the conflicts and social issues arising out of the petroleum strategy generated an intense power struggle within the state. The drama reflected the larger social conflict—albeit filtered through the prism of political–bureaucratic interests—as state managers strived to protect their political interests and to maintain the stability of the prevailing political order.

5

Defeat of the Petroleum Export Strategy: Intrabureaucratic Conflict and Policy Incoherence

Introduction

Changes in Mexico's political economy over the last forty years have generated important transformations within the Mexican state. The emphasis on industrialization is reflected in the predominance of those departments and agencies responsible for activities related to industry. As we saw in the last chapter, after 1976 and the rise of the petroleum export strategy, PEMEX—and particularly its director general—came to play a central role in economic policymaking. Policy came to rest in the hands of a political–bureaucratic elite that has become increasingly narrow in its background and support base.

This chapter explores the policy orientations and conflicts within this elite. Included in our definition of the Mexican *political elite* are the president and his personal advisory team (the Office of Economic Advisers to the President), the Economic Cabinet, the director general of PEMEX, and the *equipos* of the PEMEX chief and of each of the members of the Economic Cabinet. As the petroleum expansionist strategy gained momentum, intense opposition to PEMEX's strategy emerged and bureaucratic forces coalesced in an attempt to defeat the strategy. This ongoing power struggle was responsible for incoherence in policy, which intensified Mexico's economic problems once the price of petroleum began to slide on the international market.

Political–Bureaucratic Factors in Policy Formulation

The Mexican political elite, its roots in the aftermath of the 1910 Revolution, has changed substantially in recent years. Between 1920 and 1946 this elite—and especially the presidential 'pre-candidates'—were dominated by self-made revolutionary leaders.[1] But President Manuel Avila Camacho (1940–1946) was the last of the old revolutionaries to hold the Mexican presidency, and his cabinet was the last in which a majority of its members rose to their positions through Party ranks.[2] Since the election of Miguel Alemán, the first civilian president, top political leadership has been recruited largely from within the public bureaucracy. Typically the political bureaucrat—as distinct from the 'politico' who has risen through the Party—is of middle-class background, has a college education usually from the National University, a degree in law, and may not have held elected office. Such individuals usually have held a wide variety of positions within the public bureaucracy before achieving cabinet rank.[3] But over the past decade, still another important shift has occurred. An increasing proportion of the top political leadership now have more specialized training—in areas such as economics and public administration—obtained from private rather than public institutions, hold postgraduate degrees, and have risen up the ranks only in the narrow range of their specialization within the public bureaucracy.[4] As a consequence, policy debates have become

1 Roderic A. Camp, 'Mexican Presidential Candidates: Changes and Portents for the Future,' *Polity* 16, no. 4 (Summer 1984): 599.
2 Roderic A. Camp, 'The Cabinet and the Técnico in Mexico and the United States,' *Journal of Comparative Administration* 3, no. 2 (August 1971).
3 Raymond Vernon was the first to note the rise of the political bureaucrat (Vernon called him a 'tecnico') and the characteristics that set him or her apart from the 'politico.' *The Dilemma of Mexico's Development* (Cambridge, MA: Harvard University Press, 1963). See also James D. Cochrane, 'Mexico's New Científicos: The Díaz Ordaz Cabinet,' *Inter-American Economic Affairs* 21, no. 1 (Summer 1967); C. E. Grimes and Charles E. P. Simmons, 'Bureaucracy and Political Control in Mexico: Towards an Assessment,' *Public Administration Review* 29, no. 1 (January–February 1969).
4 Roderic A. Camp, 'The Political Technocrat in Mexico and the Survival of the Political System,' *Latin American Research Review* 20, no. 1 (1985). Camp draws a distinction between administrative bureaucrats who, although they rise within the public bureaucracy, have general training (law) and experience, as opposed to more highly trained individuals with more narrow experience

increasingly narrow, defined by specialized bureaucratic parameters.

Until recently, however, opposing interests and ideological tendencies did coexist within the postrevolutionary administrations.[5] One author has suggested that the stability of the Mexican political system has rested not on the building of institutions but on a balancing act 'based on a constantly renewed political bargain among several ruling groups and interests, representing a broad range of ideological tendencies and social bases.'[6] This arrangement had its roots in the pact reached by competing revolutionary leaders after the Mexican Revolution, that each of the competing viewpoints—the old liberalism of the 1857 Constitution and the new statism and concern for social justice—would be represented among the top political leadership. Cabinet appointments and other top advisory and administrative positions thus have been said to reflect 'the prevailing political balance.'[7] The president therefore—while the source of all benefits and rewards—has simultaneously performed the role of arbitrating and moderating the often conflicting demands emanating through his top advisers from all parts of the political system.[8]

---

whom he calls 'técnicos.' Camp has noted a similar trend among presidential precandidates, who tend more and more to have specialized training and administrative experience. Mexico's last three presidents, Echeverría, López Portillo, and de la Madrid, had not held elected office before becoming president. On this see, Roderic A. Camp, 'Mexican Presidential Candidates: Changes and Portents for the Future,' *Polity* 26, no. 4 (Summer 1984).

5 Although there were policy differences within the administration of López Portillo, these differences, we shall argue, were relatively minor. It is generally agreed that de la Madrid's team has been even more homogeneous.

6 Susan Kaufman Purcell and John F. Purcell, 'State and Society in Mexico: Must a Stable Society be Institutionalized?,' *World Politics* 30, no. 2 (January 1980): 195.

7 Peter Smith, *Labyrinths of Power* (Princeton, NJ: Princeton University Press, 1979), pp. 14 and 123. Indeed, it has been pointed out that the major sources from which the political elite have been recruited were characterized, during the 1920s and 1930s, by their ideological diversity (the National University and the National Preparatory School). Preparatory and university professors— who have played an important role in socializing and recruiting students into politics—ranged from ideologically conservative (positivist) to marxist. See, Roderic A. Camp, *The Making of Government* (Tucson: University of Arizona Press, 1984).

8 The president's role in aggregating conflicting demands has been recognized by a wide variety of scholars, many of whom do not share similar views on the nature and operation of the wider political system. See, for example, Kenneth

Today the president still performs this role, although the interests that he must accommodate are those emanating from the private sector, the public bureaucracy, and from privileged worker and middle-class groups. Cooptation occurs by means of alliances between bureaucratic groups and outside clienteles for financial gain. Particular ministries or agencies of government, responding to specific clienteles, may become important sources of policy pressure. At the same time, the fact that the president allows each of his secretaries and other top officials to appoint their own immediate subordinates reinforces competing bureaucratic interests. These *equipos* (literally, 'teams') and the alliances they form with their mainly private-sector clients outside of the public bureaucracy (known as *camarillas*) compete intensely for presidential support for their policy positions. As we saw in the previous chapter, the PEMEX camarilla's expansionist strategy won out during most of the 1976–1982 period. It has been suggested that while the president heads the 'primary camarilla,' secondary camarillas are led by his closest associates.[9] But although political bureaucrats may hold conflicting policy orientations, the system is unlikely to break down into factional bureaucratic infighting. Perhaps most importantly the overriding commitment of the political leadership to 'peace and order,' to the perpetuation and stability of the political system, ensures that even fundamental disagreements will be set aside if the political order is threatened.[10] Opposing views are mitigated by a firm commitment to collaboration among members of the political bureaucracy and a strong sense of pragmatism. Political bureaucrats operate on the basis of agreed-upon 'rules of the game' that bind the system together and ensure conflicts will be worked out.[11] Among these operating norms is the commitment to keep one's rank and file in line and to contain conflict within acceptable limits. This requirement is facilitated by the dominant

F. Johnson, *Mexican Democracy: A Critical View* (New York: Praeger, 1978), p. 66; L. Vincent Padgett, *The Mexican Political System* (Boston: Houghton Mifflin, 1976), p. 215; Martin Harry Greenberg, *Bureaucracy and Development: A Mexican Case Study* (Lexington, MA: D. C. Heath, 1970), p. 46.

9 Roderic A. Camp, *Mexico's Leaders* (Tucson: University of Arizona Press, 1980), p. 5.

10 See Roderic A. Camp, *The Making of a Government*, p. 135.

11 Peter Smith, *Labyrinths of Power*, p. 50 ff.

value of loyalty to the president. This loyalty binds together the top political leadership and works its way down the political bureaucracy, binding together individuals who have formed close friendships during their years at college or earlier and who have helped each other in their career goals.[12] Loyalty to one's superior and his goals can, as we saw in the case of the petroleum expansionist strategy, have important implications for the policy process.

Policies are also mightily influenced by an even more important aspect of intrapolitical elite relations: the presidential succession struggle. One popular conception has been that policy innovations coincide with changes in the presidency and that, with the so-called pendulum effect, presidential programs have alternated from left to right to left, from administration to administration, as presidents attempt to maintain a political balance.[13] Although data to support this theory is lacking, there does appear to be fairly clear evidence of a spending-policy cycle within, rather than between, administrations.[14] Evidence suggests that spending will increase in the second year as a new administration implements new programs and will rise again at the close of an administration as it seeks to complete projects before leaving office.[15]

The succession struggle, beginning from the moment the new cabinet is appointed at the beginning of a sexenio, sets the pattern for alliances and policy outcome. Although it is generally agreed that the president is the 'supreme elector,' his decision is not a purely personal one.[16] The succession struggle consists of a

---

12 On this, see Merilee S. Grindle, 'Patrons and Clients in the Bureaucracy: Career Networks in Mexico,' *Latin American Research Review* 12, no. 1 (1977): 40–41.

13 See for example Martin C. Needler, *Politics and Society in Mexico* (Albuquerque: University of New Mexico Press, 1971).

14 For a critique of the pendulum theory through an analysis of government expenditures, see Dale Story, 'Policy Cycles in Mexican Presidential Politics,' *Latin American Research Review* 20, no. 3 (1985).

15 Ibid., p. 154.

16 Most observers agree that some degree of consultation occurs between the president and major groups in Mexican society, since the president cannot afford to choose anyone who would provoke a severely adverse reaction. There is disagreement, however, as to the extent of this consultation. Whereas North American scholars have tended to see the process as a fairly rational one in which the president attempts to balance conflicting ideologies and interests

number of stages all of which can have important policy implications.[17] The cabinet secretaries from whom the successor is
drawn are first of all put through a series of tests to reveal their
competence in their respective ministries. Since those who fail
this test are removed from the 'running,' to be considered a
first-rate secretary of state is the primary objective of any aspi-
rant. It is perhaps in part for this reason that the technocrat has
become so important. A technically competent secretary, or one
that performs competently because of good advice from his
'equipo,' has the best hope of clearing this first hurdle, especially
in the economic portfolios. The next 'test,' occurring during the
third and fourth years of the sexenio, demands a demonstration
of ability in political management and conciliation—that is, proof
one has knowledge of the 'rules of the game.' The final phase,
during the fifth year, occurs once the president has designated
who the precandidates are. This period is characterized by
intense political maneuvering as the president tries to gauge the
ability of each precandidate to establish a public image and to deal
with the media and public issues. During this time the president
likewise tries to measure public support for each precandidate.
The process is clearly geared for the emergence of a 'man of the
system,' one who is highly disciplined in the rules of the game
and dedicated to their preservation.

Especially during the early part of the sexenio, then,
bureaucratic–technical administrative teams clash as presidential
aspirants attempt to show they are efficient servants of the president and to demonstrate the correctness of their policies. As
competing teams pressure the president for support of their
respective programs, policy inconsistency may result as the
president is swayed by one team or another or implements contradictory parts of each program. In later years, as it becomes
important for presidential aspirants to demonstrate support and
'political management,' policy struggles will become increasingly
oriented toward the satisfaction of respective clienteles. Secreta-

---

in his choice, Mexican scholars have tended to see the process as much more
capricious. See for example Daniel Cosío Villegas, *La sucesión presidencial*
(México, D.F.: Editorial Joaquín Mortiz, 1975).

17 These stages are outlined in Rubén Narvaez, *La sucesión presidencial* (México,
D.F.: Instituto Mexicano de Sociologia Política, A.C., 1981).

ries must strengthen their political bases through expanding government spending to satisfy these clienteles.

Between 1976 and 1982 these political–bureaucratic factors interacted with distinct policy orientations, determining the pattern of policy outcome. During this period three economic strategies struggled for predominance. Chapter 3 has dealt at some length with the most successful of these strategies: the expansionist strategy. We now turn to a discussion of the other two bureaucratic policy orientations that competed with the expansionist strategy for predominance. Here we shall focus upon the manner in which these policy orientations interacted with political–bureaucratic factors in the determination of policy.

Bureaucratic Policy Tendencies in the Policymaking Process

While the expansionist strategy was centred in PEMEX, two other tendencies—the neoliberal and the quasi-populist—were represented in the Economic Cabinet. We have referred to these policy positions as 'tendencies' or 'orientations' in order to reflect the fact that they do not represent pure, distinct types; rather, they represent extremes on a continuum. Nor are the policy orientations of Mexican political bureaucrats closely identifiable with particular schools of economic thought as a number of observers have suggested.[18] There is broad agreement among political bureaucrats on fundamentals. All believe in the need for industrialization and in the necessity of measures to encourage the private sector, particularly the most powerful financial and industrial groups. Most agree that the state should have an important role in the economy and that essential areas, such as petroleum, electricity, and transportation, should be in government hands.

During the early López Portillo years, the political bureaucracy was generally agreed on a number of aspects of economic policy. All supported petroleum exploitation and exportation to overcome the economic crisis of the mid-1970s. There was disagreement, however, over the use of petroleum dollars and the continued

---

18 See for example, *The New York Times* (October 24, 1982): 13.

rise of production levels once the crisis had been overcome.

The policy debates that occurred took place within the framework of a general agreement on a capital-intensive, high-technology strategy. The old populist *agrarista* option was not even under consideration.[19] Although it was recognized that job creation ought to be an objective of government policy, there was no policy debate surrounding the overall impact of the government's economic program on inequality or on the rural sector. Even the quasi-populist tendency within the political bureaucracy did not share the old populist concern for the agricultural sector, which had been the center piece in the heyday of Mexican populism under Cárdenas and had undergone a resurgence under Echeverría. A new technocratic populism had arisen which ignored the political aspects of traditional Mexican populism.[20] This policy tendency did, however, show some concern for selective redistribution and for the expansion and protection of the domestic market. Although we may speak of political bureaucrats who express greater concern for government spending and excessive state intervention in the economy than other political bureaucrats, in this context the term *neoliberal* does not imply Mexico's version of the 'Chicago boys.' Although this bureaucratic faction shared certain views with the neoclassical school, we cannot speak of a wholesale devotion to the free flow of market forces.

The Quasi-Populist Tendency

The quasi-populist faction proved to be Díaz Serrano's most formidable opponent during the period. Centered largely in the Ministry of Natural Resources and Industrial Development, its

---

19 As demonstrated by López Portillo's dismissal of his agrarian reform secretary, Jorge Rojo Lugo, a known supporter of continued land redistribution. This policy option was rejected by the president because, in his view, there was no more land to redistribute, and because such a policy did not get at the root of the agrarian problem, the need to increase productivity. *Unomásuno* (27 Noviembre 1977): 3. The new agrarian reform secretary, Antonio Toledo Corro, was a member of a powerful Sinaloan landholding family with connections to multinational agribusiness.

20 Such as political incorporation of the poor, especially the rural poor.

[94]

most prominent spokesman was that department's secretary, José Andrés de Oteyza. But the tendency was also found in other parts of the government: the Ministry of Budget and Planning (or SPP, as it is commonly known), especially during Carlos Tello's tenure as secretary in 1977; and it was probably predominant in the Office of Economic Advisers to the President.

This tendency is commonly associated with the interventionist philosophy espoused by a group of economists at Cambridge University. Certainly there appears to have been close personal ties between university economists and key members of this bureaucratic faction. Both the secretary of natural resources and the director general (Natán Warman) of the Institute of Industrial Planning (within the same ministry) were students at Cambridge, as was Carlos Tello, briefly secretary of budget and planning and later head of the Central Bank and the nationalized banking sector. While its opponents argue that the influence of the Cambridge economists was great, it should be born in mind that many of the attitudes expressed by this bureaucratic faction, such as strong state intervention, had long been present within the Mexican leadership. At most, Cambridge theories reinforced and gave intellectual legitimacy to this tendency.

This policy orientation favored an activist role for the state in economic planning and improving living standards.[21] Here we see a concern for the social implications of economic policy, at least insofar as it affected sectors represented by organized and powerful trade unions. One of the most important objectives of economic policy was the creation of employment; this aim was to be achieved by means of petroleum development, which was to propel a high growth rate of between 8 and 10 percent.[22] Another essential ingredient of this strategy was a healthy growth rate in

---

21 For a good discussion of this policy orientation, see Vladimiro Brailovsky, 'Industrialization and Oil in Mexico: A Long-term perspective,' in Terry Barker and Vladimiro Brailovsky, eds., *Oil or Industry?* (London: Academic Press, 1981). The National Industrial Development Plan and the Energy Program also reflect this perspective. See Sepafin, *Plan nacional de desarrollo industrial, 1979–1982*; and idem, *Programa de energía: Metas a 1990 y proyecciones al año 2000*.

22 The National Industrial Development Plan called for a growth rate of 9.5 percent for 1981 and 10.5 percent in 1982. However, by the time the energy program was published in November of 1980, the growth objective had been scaled down to 8 percent in 1981 and 1982.

public investment. Hence proponents of this policy opposed the 1976 IMF stabilization program and resisted austerity measures in 1981 and 1982 after the price of petroleum had declined on the international market. PEMEX's high rate of expansion was opposed on two grounds. First, the very high production levels being advocated by the expansionist strategy had necessitated a high level of importation of machinery, equipment, and other inputs. The decline in protection for indigenous firms was opposed as protection was seen as essential to long-term employment prospects. Second, PEMEX's ever-expanding development program was taking up too large a proportion of the budget. Holders of this perspective were not so much concerned about the level of government expenditure as about the direction of that expenditure.[23] The quasi-populist tendency advocated a more diversified investment program, especially in industries such as steel, petrochemicals, and capital goods. It also echoed the views of Mexico's nationalist left, expressing concern for Mexico's vulnerability as a petroleum export economy and seeking to reduce dependence on petroleum exports through a program stimulating manufacturing exports. This perspective assumed that high growth rates were compatible with equilibrium in the balance of payments as long as imports and capital outflows were strictly controlled. It was argued that measures such as increased taxes could help improve the balance of payments by reducing the requirements for foreign borrowing. This bureaucratic faction opposed devaluation as a solution, arguing that the impact of such a measure would be largely on the level of domestic demand.

Within the quasi-populist perspective there were different emphases depending upon the institutional and clientelistic interests of bureaucrats, and both the interests of institutions and clienteles played a central role in the patterning of this and other bureaucratic policy orientations. Both the Ministry of Natural Resources and Industrial Development and the Ministry of Budget and Planning had functions and clienteles that predi-

---

23 Proponents of this perspective claim that they do not regard government spending as providing a long-term solution; rather, they argue that at certain times it may be of some short-term assistance.

sposed them to a statist position. Responsible for both industrial development and the enormous parastate sector, officials of the Ministry of Natural Resources and Industrial Development had a vested interest in protecting industry (the ministry's clientele) and in expanding the state's participation in the economy. Indeed, the Ministry of Natural Resources and Industrial Development has a tradition of supporting interventionist policies. It tends as a consequence to recruit disproportionately economists with a more statist bent. Those, who upon entering the ministry do not share this viewpoint, tend to become socialized in the goals of the institution and acquire a statist viewpoint more coincident with their career interests.

The policy orientation of the Ministry of Budget and Planning was also reflective of its institutional interests and functions. Established in 1977, professionals were drawn from four departments: Finance, Natural Resources, Industry and Commerce, and the Office of the Presidency.[24] This ministry was given the responsibility of formulating the national and regional plans for economic and social development, of developing an annual budget of investment and expenditure for the federal government and parastates, and of evaluating the results of all programs. Despite the heterogeneity of its recruitment base, and despite frequent changes in secretaries and top administrative teams with widely varying policy orientations, the ministry presented a surprisingly consistent policy orientation.[25] As the ministry responsible for economic planning, the SPP remained heavily statist throughout the period. As the ministry responsible for the development of the budget and, as a consequence, subject to pressure from all parts of the federal bureaucracy, it remained a strong supporter of expansionary government spending even when its secretary, Miguel de la Madrid, was a fiscal conser-

---

24 For SPP's origins and functions, see SPP, *Informes de labores*, Período de 1 de Septiembre de 1976 a 31 de Agosto 1977, México, D.F., 1979; and SPP 'Avances de programa de reforma administrativa' México, D.F. (Junio 1980).

25 The Ministry of Budget and Planning had four different secretaries between 1976 and 1982. While the first, Secretary Carlos Tello, resigned due to his opposition to a tight spending program, Miguel de la Madrid, secretary between May 1979 and September 1981, was a known fiscal conservative.

vative.[26] With a broader mandate than any other ministry, Budget and Planning became concerned about the broad social and economic implications of the rapid exploitation of petroleum, such as its impact on agriculture and regional discontent.[27] This concern—plus the desire to direct more government revenue away from petroleum and into other sectors of the economy—brought it directly into opposition with PEMEX's expansionary program.

But differences over policy reinforced by distinct clientelistic interests were not the only factors behind the opposition of the quasi-populists to PEMEX's expansionist strategy. The opposition also reflected a bitter power struggle as these secretaries resisted PEMEX's encroachment upon their decision-making authority. The most bitter conflict occurred between the director general of PEMEX, Díaz Serrano, and the secretary of natural resources, José Andrés de Oteyza. While in theory PEMEX was under the authority of the secretary of natural resources, in fact the director general—by virtue of his knowledge of the petroleum industry, the success of his program, and his very close friendship with the president—bypassed the secretary and reported directly to the president. PEMEX's autonomy also pitted it against the Ministry of Budget and Planning, which could neither get information from it nor force it to mesh its plans with those of other departments and agencies.[28] PEMEX's monopolization of the budget made it difficult for Budget and Planning to attend to the multitude of pressures exerted upon it for government monies. For Budget and Planning and for the Ministry of Natural Resources, stopping PEMEX became the overriding concern.

26 During the sexenio, de la Madrid appeared to undergo an ideological metamorphosis of sorts. From being one of the chief spokesmen for restrictive budgeting policies as deputy secretary of finance at the end of 1977, he became, in his new position as secretary for budget and planning, a strong proponent of a government program to promote employment and consumption and for increased state participation in the expansion of goals and services. See, *Tiempo* 76, núm. 1959 (19 Noviembre 1979): 18.

27 SPP's 'Programa de acción del sector público 1978–1982' expressed concern for the 'profound crisis' being experienced by the agricultural sector (Segunda Parte, p. 3.). See also Primara Parte, p. 37 ff.

28 An internal study of PEMEX by the Ministry of Budget and Planning claimed that PEMEX was 'administratively chaotic, financially insolvent and politically autonomous.' *Proceso*, núm. 238 (25 de Mayo 1981): 6.

The fact that decisions pertaining to petroleum were not put before the Economic Cabinet aroused the hostility of most secretaries. There was also some concern over Díaz Serrano's presidential aspirations. Díaz Serrano was generally regarded as an outsider tainted by his connections with American multinationals. It was as a consequence all the more important to put an end to PEMEX's expansionary program, for such a defeat would put an end to its director general's presidential aspirations.

The Neoliberal Tendency

This tendency was centered in the Ministry of Finance and in the Central Bank. Traditionally the most powerful ministry because of its control over both revenue and the allocation of expenditure (until the creation of Budget and Planning in 1977), the Ministry of Finance in the early 1920s embraced the belief that development necessitated the creation of a strong national bourgeoisie.[29] The common outlook shared by middle- and high-level technocrats both in Finance and the Central Bank—and in *Nacional Financiera* (Mexico's industrial development bank)—can be traced to an in-house training program developed in the Bank.[30] A high level of personnel continuity was also present in the finance sector.[31] Hence a distinct institutional outlook reinforced formal powers.

Finance officials are usually regarded as the most conservative within the Mexican political bureaucracy and the least concerned with the social implications of economic policy. The finance ministry was the architect of the stabilizing development program that, as we saw, produced healthy growth rates at the cost of growing inequality.

Beginning in the late 1950s the finance ministry began to lose

---

29 Douglas Bennett and Kenneth Sharpe, 'The State as Banker and Entrepreneur: The Last Resort Character of Mexico's State Intervention, 1917–1970,' in Sylvia Ann Hewlett and Richard Weinert, eds., *Brazil and Mexico: Patterns of Late Development* (Philadelphia: Institute for the Study of Human Issues, 1982), p. 175.

30 Ibid., p. 177.

31 John J. Bailey, 'Presidency, Bureaucracy and Administrative Reform in Mexico: The Secretariat of Program and Budgeting,' *Inter-American Economic Affairs* 34 (Summer 1980): 35.

power, and its decline was roughly commensurate with the rise of the Ministry of Natural Resources and Industrial Development. In 1947, responsibility for the administration of industrial parastates was taken away from the Ministry of Finance and given to the newly created ministry of *National Property*. An administrative reorganization during the administration of Adolfo López Mateos (1958–1964) gave the Ministry of Natural Resources control over the parastate sector and created the Ministry of the Presidency, responsible for formulating national plans and approving investment spending.[32] President Echeverría further challenged the Ministry of Finance's dominance by his movement of expenditure decisions to the Ministry of the Presidency and by his strengthening of the Ministry of Natural Resources through increasing the size and complexity of its investments.

It has been suggested that the earlier neoclassicism of finance officials had been watered down by the impact of the Cárdenas period.[33] Although concerned with the efficiency of state enterprises, privatization was not a central worry. The belief that a dominant state presence in such areas as petroleum, electricity, and mining is vital is evidence of a commitment to a strong state role. Finance officials did not demonstrate complete faith in the free flow of market forces: they opposed Mexico's entry into the General Agreement on Trade and Tariffs (GATT) during the administration of López Portillo and have favored policies to stimulate the capital goods industry as this would help Mexico's balance of payments situation. As one official schooled in the neoclassical tradition put it, 'Milton Friedman's theories are fine in the United States . . . but when you're here working with Mexican problems you begin to see things differently. The circumstances and the culture are different.' Finance officials claim

---

32 The formation of the Ministry of the Presidency followed a failed attempt to create a Ministry of Budget and Planning. Minutes before the bill was to be sent to Congress, the name was changed to 'Ministry of the Presidency' and it was deprived of the ability to intervene in the preparation of current and capital budgets and left only with the responsibility of planning and coordinating investment programs.

33 Douglas Bennett and Kenneth Sharpe, 'The State as Banker and Entrepreneur: The Last Resort Character of the Mexican State's Intervention, 1917–1970,' p. 177.

that they are not contractionists, and they have not agreed entirely with International Monetary Fund prescriptions for economic recovery.[34] They argue however that development programs must be 'properly financed.' Claiming not to have been opposed in principle to an expansionary program after 1976, they nonetheless still believed that the debt and the public deficit ought to have been solved before such a program was embarked upon.

It was precisely on those issues most closely tied to the finance sector's institutional functions that its attitudes most closely resembled the IMF position. Responsible for the raising of revenue and for monetary policy, the primary concerns of Finance and Central Bank officials were the public deficit, foreign debt, and inflation. Rapid petroleum exploitation and rapid growth rates (8 percent was considered excessive) were opposed by finance officials as such policies would create too much demand for imports, generate too much government spending and foreign borrowing, and stimulate inflation, all of which would undermine business confidence. Finance had urged support for the 1976 IMF stabilization program and from 1979 urged the government to cut back on public spending and borrowing. Support for the petroleum development program had been given in the hope that petroleum sales—while improving the balance of payments—would also contribute to a reduction in the growth of the public debt. When policy continued to be expansionary, as government spending and the debt rapidly grew, the finance ministry allied with the quasi-populists to put an end to PEMEX's expansionary program.

Finance's commitment to hold down government expenditure, reduce the growth of the debt, and control inflation was very much a reflection of its mandate within the federal bureaucracy. Because of its specific concerns, it has tended to attract economists with neoclassical training. As the ministry responsible for the negotiation of government loans, it has had frequent intermittent contact with the International Monetary Fund and other

---

34 While they have agreed that government spending has been Mexico's major problem, they have resisted the severity of the cutbacks recommended by the IMF.

international lending agencies. No doubt such close contact has stimulated a likemindedness reflected in the fact that the finance ministry, like the IMF, has blamed government spending for Mexico's economic difficulties.

The clientele of the government's financial bureaucracy has been private banking, and its constant contact with this very powerful private sector undoubtedly reinforced a similarity of perspective. The relationship between top finance officials and the most powerful private bankers has been historically direct and close. The Bank of Mexico (before the Bank nationalization of 1982) was owned jointly by the federal government (owning 51 percent of its capital) and by the private banking sector (owning 49 percent of its shares). This gave the private banking sector four representatives on the administrative council of the Bank of Mexico while the government had five. Private banking was thus able to participate directly in decisions regarding interest rates and legal reserve requirements and was afforded a point of access by which its views were filtered through the political bureaucracy. Finance's institutional concerns over inflation and government spending were thus reinforced by similar private-sector concerns. Institutional interests and clientelistic ties were, then, critical in the shaping of discernible policy orientations.

By 1979 the most powerful members of López Portillo's Economic Cabinet—Natural Resources and Budget and Planning, on the one hand, and Finance and the Central Bank, on the other—motivated by distinct interests and representing opposing policy orientations, joined together to put an end to PEMEX's expansionist drive.[35]

Intense opposition to PEMEX's expansionist strategy also came from the Office of Economic Advisers to the President. From this office came concerns about the appropriate use of petroleum dollars and the danger of overheating the economy. It was only here, from the president's adviser on agricultural matters, Cassio Luiselli, that serious worries were voiced over the state of the

---

35 While no discernible policy orientation emanated from the Ministry of Commerce, it too came to oppose the raising of the production ceiling. It was concerned about the declining importance of manufactured goods and agricultural products as a proportion of total exports. It was the only ministry to support Mexico's entry into GATT at this time.

agricultural sector. Stemming from urgings of the agricultural adviser of this group, a self-sufficiency program known as SAM (the Mexican Food System) was initiated. Convincing the president, however, was only half the battle as the program met stiff resistance from top officials who saw no reason why the generous flow of petroleum dollars could not be used to purchase food needs.[36] It was the prestigious, high-technology projects that were most likely to be supported and funded.

As industrialization has taken its course, vested interests tied to industry, both within the state and outside, have become increasingly important. The expansion of peripheral industrialization has been reflected in the rising importance of the Ministries of Natural Resources and Industrial Development, of Nafinsa (Mexico's industrial development bank), and more recently of PEMEX along with the growing importance of each of their respective clienteles. The decline in the importance of those ministries traditionally staffed by the PRI, such as Agriculture and Agrarian Reform,[37] has been coincident with the rising importance of industry and the bureaucratic organizations concerned with this activity.

Intrabureaucratic Infighting and Policy Incoherence

The major issue around which conflict revolved before 1981 was that of the petroleum production ceiling; this struggle pitted the expansionists against the quasi-populists and neoliberals. The issues of levels of government spending and public debt divided the quasi-populists and neoliberals throughout the period but never became as divisive as the question of the petroleum production ceiling. The period was characterized by intense lobbying of the president by each of these factions.

---

36 There were two central pieces of agricultural legislation during the period: the 1981 Law to Stimulate Agriculture and the Mexican Food System (S.A.M.). Both sought to avoid further land redistribution through subsidies and guaranteed prices to farmers. Through 'superior forms of organization,' S.A.M. sought to increase minifundia and ejidal efficiency.

37 Steven E. Sanderson, 'Presidential Succession and Political Rationality in Mexico,' *World Politics* 35 (April 1983): 319.

Under IMF restrictions during 1977 and 1978, and aided by the low momentum in government spending that accompanies the first year of any sexenio, the president acceded to the arguments of the neoliberal faction that resistance to an immediate and large expansion in government expenditure and wage demands would help restore business confidence. Hence, while policies during the first two years of López Portillo's administration by no means followed a strict stabilization program, they were certainly more restrictive than in later years. The public deficit, at 6.7 percent of GDP for 1977 and 1978, was lower than in later years.[38] Minimum wages increased by only 10 percent in 1977 and 12 percent in 1978, while inflation was held at 30 percent and 10 percent respectively. The deficit on the current account was reduced in 1977, although it rose again steadily after 1978.[39]

But despite the absence of strict adherence to IMF prescriptions, the quasi-populists were convinced that the president had been won over by the neoliberal line. This fact precipitated the then secretary of budget and planning, Carlos Tello, to quit the government; his letter of resignation spoke of the necessity to 'promote production and employment and rectify the contradictory policy put in place by finance ministry officials supported by the IMF.'[40]

After 1979 however the pendulum began to swing in the direction of the expansionists and the quasi-populists. Few of the concerns expressed by the neoliberals—about the negative impact of high growth rates, the increasing government deficit and the debt on inflation, worries over undermining business confidence—found expression in government policy after 1979. SPP's *Programa de acción del sector público (1978–1982)* announced

---

38 See Appendix Table 3.1. The IMF target for 1977 was 6 percent, and for 1978, 4 percent. Government policies in 1977 and 1978, given their nonrestrictive nature, have been called by one observer 'an escape from IMF prescriptions.' Laurence Whitehead, 'Mexico from Bust to Boom: A Political Evaluation of the 1976–1979 Stabilization Program,' *World Development* 8, no. 11 (November 1980): 851.

39 See Appendix Table 1.4.

40 *Unomásuno* (18 de Noviembre 1977): 2. The president was then forced to ask for the resignation of his finance secretary, Moctezuma Cid, in order not to appear to be siding with the more restrictive, and less popular, policies of the neoliberal faction.

that starting with 1979 a progressive increase of average salary would be initiated.[41] The quasi-populist's goal of a fast growth rate was pursued. With petroleum as the axle of growth, the National Industrial Development Plan, released in April 1979, called for a growth rate of 7 percent in 1979, 9.5 percent in 1981, and 10.5 percent for 1982. Growth was to be propelled by state-led investment projects financed through oil earnings. By 1979 the commitment to government budget restraint had been dropped. But the quasi-populists, distressed that ever larger amounts of capital were continuing to go into the petroleum industry, pushed for the channeling of funds into other projects. This faction was also the leading opponent of Mexico's entry into GATT. In the minds of the quasi-populists the expansionist petroleum strategy and GATT were linked. The pursuit of the expansionist strategy combined with Mexico's entry into GATT would relegate Mexico to the position of a monoexport, primary-production economy, severely increasing its dependence on the United States.[42] It was the spokesman for the quasi-populist faction—the secretary of natural resources and industrial development, de Oteyza—who led the campaign to put an end to PEMEX's expansionism and to Díaz Serrano's presidential aspirations. He easily won support from the other secretaries who were becoming increasingly uneasy at the impact of PEMEX's expansionism. As pointed out, the finance ministry and the Central Bank were especially concerned about the level of public spending and debt.

The intrabureaucratic battle over the petroleum production ceiling was waged between September 1979 and March 1980, triggered by Díaz Serrano's presentation of a report to the Economic Cabinet recommending that the production ceiling targeted for 1982 be raised from 2.25 million barrels per day to 4 million barrels. In response the Economic Cabinet established a

41 SPP, 'Programa de acción del sector público, 1978–1982,' p. 89.

42 The major exponent of entry into GATT within the political bureaucracy was the Ministry of Commerce and, in the private sector, those organizations representing the most powerful financial–industrial interests. However, these private-sector interests conceded that entry into GATT was not essential as long as Mexico had petroleum 'as an instrument of negotiation.' See *Razones*, núm. 11 (2–15 Junio, 1980): 22 ff. The issue was not a particularly contentious one at this time and commerce was easily defeated in cabinet.

'technical commission' composed of senior-level officials from the ministries of the Economic Cabinet. Not surprisingly, the report produced by the technical commission strongly urged that the production ceiling not be raised. While the president was deliberating on this and the PEMEX report, a period of intense lobbying ensued, with both sides holding frequent personal interviews with the president. The president was finally persuaded to hold down the petroleum production ceiling only with the united opposition of all members of the Economic Cabinet; they sent a joint letter to the President stating their opposition to any further increase in the production ceiling. Although the president was apparently personally inclined in the direction of the expansionist strategy, he could not allow it to continue in the face of the combined hostility of his most powerful cabinet secretaries. Hence, when the president in his speech of March 1980 limited petroleum production to 2.5 million barrels per day plus 10 percent, it was greeted as a victory by the Economic Cabinet.[43] Indeed the stiff bureaucratic resistance to the priority given the petroleum industry by the president may account for the discrepancy between the proportion of the budget originally authorized for PEMEX and that actually spent. In 1980, other parastates were able to increase their actual expenditure above originally authorized amounts at PEMEX's expense.[44]

During the dispute—and even after it was supposedly resolved—this intense intrabureaucratic infighting was reflected in policy incoherence. Government officials contradicted each other at every turn. For many months it was not at all clear whether Mexico had a petroleum production ceiling or not.[45] While Díaz Serrano continued to state publicly that the petroleum

---

43 It was at this time that the president also announced that Mexico would not enter GATT and that an attempt would be made to resuscitate the agricultural sector through the new S.A.M. program.

44 See Appendix Table 3.4.

45 In 1979 Díaz Serrano flatly contradicted the president's earlier reassertion of a production ceiling of 2.25 million barrels per day, announcing publicly that Mexico's petroleum policy was being reviewed 'to see if 4 million barrels per day could not be produced by 1982.' *Latin America Daily Report* 6, no. 19 (January 26, 1979): m1; *Latin American Economic Report* 7, no. 11 (March 16, 1979): 81. However, by 1980 the president announced to foreign journalists that a decision on the petroleum ceiling was pending. *International Petroleum Times* (January 1980): 12.

production ceiling would have to be raised for PEMEX to fulfill the contracts that were being negotiated, the president flatly refuted him.[46] Finally, Díaz Serrano was forced to reverse himself. He and the secretary of natural resources and industrial development held a press conference to clarify matters, during which they jointly announced that recently negotiated export sales would not entail any alteration in the production ceiling.[47] Then in May of 1981—following the March presidential announcement that the petroleum production ceiling would not be raised—PEMEX published its 'Program of Operation,' which clearly violated the official petroleum plan: it called for production of 2.9 million barrels per day by July of 1981. It was by now clear that neither PEMEX's bureaucratic opponents nor the president had been able to put an end to PEMEX's expansionary strategy. The strategy of rapid petroleum development had acquired a momentum of its own, pushed relentlessly forward by the powerful PEMEX technocracy. The matter was finally resolved not by executive decision but by international events. The drop of petroleum prices on the international market not only removed much of the incentive for increased production but also precipitated the exit of its strongest proponent, Jorge Díaz Serrano.

The drop of petroleum prices on the international market in the spring of 1981 gave Díaz Serrano's enemies within the political bureaucracy the opportunity they had been waiting for to achieve their ultimate goals: securing the director general's exit and his definitive removal as a presidential precandidate. The ensuing bureaucratic battle produced an irrational pricing policy that exacerbated Mexico's economic problems. Not an expert in the international petroleum market, Díaz Serrano had been dependent upon a small number of PEMEX technocrats for advice in this area. Aware of the softening of demand for hydrocarbons, these technocrats had been pressing him for some time to lower

---

46 In fact, a letter of intent from PEMEX to the United States made the future sale of increased amounts of petroleum to the United States conditional upon raising the production ceiling. *Proceso*, núm. 84 (2 de Julio 1980): 34; *Unomásuno* (25 de Mayo 1980): 1.

47 *Latin American Weekly Report* (June 13, 1980): 4; *Proceso*, núm. 187 (2 de Julio 1980): 25.

Mexico's international prices. But it was not until June of 1981—after petroleum prices had already begun to fall in May—that Díaz Serrano was persuaded to lower the price of mixed light and heavy crude, which Mexico sold on the international market at $4 a barrel. This decision, PEMEX technocrats argued, was necessary to retain customers. A great deal of nationalist furor was stirred up around the issue. The secretary of natural resources, José Andrés de Oteyza, spoke of the decision as 'cheapening the patrimony of the people.'[48] On the pretext that the decision had been taken arbitrarily and without consulting the president, Díaz Serrano was forced to resign on June 3. Although it is likely that the president was in fact consulted, the Economic Cabinet was not. The issue became not the correctness of the decision but the ongoing power struggle between the secretary of natural resources, de Oteyza, and the PEMEX chief.

Having engineered Díaz Serrano's demise over the issue of the reduction of petroleum prices (de Oteyza's position was that Díaz Serrano was selling off Mexico's resources too cheaply), the secretary of natural resources now had to make right the situation by raising those prices. Hence, by the end of June, PEMEX announced a $2-a-barrel increase backdated to July 1 and a reduction in production. In the face of a falling international market for petroleum, several countries suspended their purchases of Mexican crude, including France; it suspended purchases of 100,000 barrels per day.[49]

By early July oil exports had dropped to an estimated 700,000 barrels per day—that is, one-half of the usual daily 1.5 million barrels;[50] the revenue loss was estimated at several billion dollars.[51] By early August Mexico abandoned the attempt to raise its price $2 and was able to regain former clients by month's end.[52]

48 *El Día* (17 de Junio 1981): 1.
49 The fiasco threatened relations with France when de Oteyza, in retaliation, threatened the termination of government contracts with various French companies involved in the building of the Mexico City subway and of reactors for Mexico's nuclear program. The matter was resolved when France agreed to resume the purchase of 100,000 barrels of crude per day.
50 *Financial Times* (July 8, 1981): 9.
51 *Financial Times* (July 7, 1981): 5.
52 The new price of Mexican oil averaged about $30.60 (U.S.) a barrel, up just 10 cents from the June average price of $30.50. *Wall Street Journal* (August 15, 1981): 3.

Conclusions

Institutional and clientelistic interests appear to have been instrumental in patterning bureaucratic policy tendencies. The policy orientations of the quasi-populists and the neoliberals appear to be directly related to institutional functions reinforced by clientelistic interests. Those specific institutional interests were further reinforced by the loyalty of bureaucrats to their superiors and by the commitment of bureaucrats to enhance the goals of those superiors. All of these policy orientations were largely technocratic in nature. The institutional and clientelistic interests that predominate in the policymaking process are those tied to capital-intensive industrialization. Although differing on the question of the rapidity of petroleum development, all bureaucratic factions were united in their commitment to a capital-intensive form of industrialization and in their general neglect of the interests of small and ejidal agriculture. With the process of rapid industrialization that had occurred in Mexico over the last forty years, peasants were no longer an important clientele. No one within the highest echelons of power articulated their demands even in a symbolic sense.[53]

Moreover, the conflict over policy has to be viewed within the framework of the presidential succession struggle. From a contest over the efficacy of programs, the bureaucratic infighting heated up to a full-scale power struggle in which antiexpansionists aimed to demonstrate to the president that Díaz Serrano was not presidential material. Díaz Serrano's presidential aspirations, his infringement on the authority of other secretaries, his advocacy of a program that conflicted with the political, bureaucratic, and clientelistic interests of other secretaries caused the formation of a tactical alliance between normally opposing bureaucratic tendencies.

---

53 The achievements of S.A.M. remain a topic of considerable debate. While its supporters point to the fact that the 1980 harvests in basic foods were 14 percent higher than the previous year—and in 1981, 19 percent higher—its detractors argue that this improvement was largely due to climactic factors. *Razones*, núm. 56 (22 Febrero–7 Marzo 1982): 11; *Latin American Weekly Report* (November 5, 1981): 9. For an assessment of S.A.M., see Steven Sanderson, *The Transformation of Mexican Agriculture* (Princeton, NJ: Princeton University Press, 1986), p. 257 ff.

But it was only with great difficulty and perhaps more due to international circumstances that PEMEX's expansionism was finally halted. Petroleum development, which had reoriented the Mexican economy, had become reflected in an important change in the power structure of the state. The powerful petroleum technocracy was perpetuating its program and eluding central control.

The political–bureaucratic elite was not involved in a process of mediating the conflicting interests of classes or class factions. Rather, the particular interests of private-sector clientelistic groups reinforced opposing bureaucratic policy tendencies. Factions of capital, although linked organically to each other, have distinct concerns and priorities and have been able to find different points of access to the state. The powerful private-banking sector—concerned about the level of government spending, the public debt, and inflation—found ready access through the Central Bank and the Ministry of Finance. Private and public industrial enterprises, whose owners and managers were troubled by foreign competition and the level of imports, found a receptive ear in the Ministry of Natural Resources and Industrial Development, while the private sector tied most closely to the petroleum industry shared a tight mutuality of interest with PEMEX.[54] As the economic crisis deepened and as bureaucratic infighting increasingly surfaced openly, policy incoherence—such as that occurring over the petroleum production ceiling and price policy—would become ever more apparent, exacerbating Mexico's economic crisis and deepening social tensions.

---

54 The attitudes of the private sector will be dealt with in more detail in the following chapter.

6

Debt and Economic Crisis

Introduction

By the end of 1982 Mexico faced its most severe economic crisis since the Great Depression. The country that in 1981 was the fourth-largest oil producer witnessed in the next year a fall of gross domestic product of −1.5 percent and an inflation rate of over 100 percent. With a foreign debt of almost $84 billion—second only to Brazil's—and its foreign-exchange reserves almost exhausted, Mexico signed an agreement with the International Monetary Fund in November of 1982; it committed the country to a strict austerity program in return for a loan of $4 billion.

The 1982 economic crisis resulted from the interaction between a particular set of external and internal circumstances. It was also, as has been argued earlier, the product of historical trends. Those critics who have emphasized the importance of internal factors behind the 1982 crisis have usually focused on the 'policy errors' made by the López Portillo administration: a too-rapid pursuit of the petroleum export strategy, a failure to take adequate measures inhibiting imports, the maintenance of an overvalued peso, an uncontrolled expansion in government expenditure, and a failure to follow policies that would have maintained the confidence of the private sector or would otherwise have prevented the outflow of capital.[1] Not only did the state fail to take decisions to alleviate the crisis, its decisions actually caused

---

1 María Elena Cardero and José Manuel Quijano, 'Expansión y estrangulamiento financiera, 1978–1982,' in *Economía mexicana*, núm. 4 (1982); Pascal Garcia-Alba and Jaime Serra-Puche, *Financial Aspects of Macro-Economic Management* (Tokyo: Institute of Developing Economies, No. 36, 1984); Leopoldo Solís and Ernesto Zedillo, 'The Foreign Debt of Mexico,' in Gordon W. Smith and John T. Cuddington, eds., *International Debt and the Developing Countries* (Washington, DC: World Bank, 1985).

further strain. The various adjustment programs instituted to deal with the economic crisis were inconsistent, swinging from continued expansion with minor accommodations to a more orthodox restrictive program. Moreover, specific policies were contradictory, vacillating between restrictive and expansionary measures. While the government was clearly unable to impose adherence to a restrictive program, neither was it able to use vigorous state intervention to stem the massive outflow of capital that its continued state-led expansionary program had produced.

External and Internal Factors in the Economic Crisis

The 1982 economic crisis, like the boom of 1976–1981, was very much linked to international events. Between the mid-1970s and 1980 Mexico had benefited from the rise in petroleum prices, the excess liquidity of international capital markets, and the intense competition between international banks for the placement of funds and consequent lower interest rates. The usual explanation for this excess liquidity is the recycling of petroleum dollars as a result of the surge in petroleum prices occurring in the mid-1970s. However, things took a turn for the worse when, between 1980 and 1982, not only did prices of crude oil and other commodities decline on the international market[2] but interest rates on loans contracted in the Euromarket with floating rates increased. The industrialized countries, undergoing one of their worst recessionary periods, resorted to protectionism, a practice that hurt the exports of manufactured goods coming from countries such as Mexico. In the face of these difficulties, and especially in the case of Mexico with the decline of petroleum prices, banks became unwilling to renew their financial support.

While the Mexican foreign debt increased throughout the 1976–1982 period, growth of the debt accelerated after 1979 and was particularly rapid during the latter part of 1981 for the public

---

2 For data on the decline in Mexico's terms of trade, see Appendix, Table 1.3. In 1981 the index of the commercial terms of trade for developing nonpetroleum countries was the lowest since 1950. José Juan De Olloqui, 'Un enfoque bancario sobre la crisis mexicana de pagos en 1982,' *El trimestre económico* LI, núm. 3 (Julio–Septiembre 1984): 530.

sector. In 1981 the total external debt of the public sector increased by $19 billion, half of which was short-term debt. The proportion of the foreign public debt accounted for by short-term debt rose from 4.4 to 20.3 percent from 1980 to 1981.[3] A dramatic jump of the public foreign debt as a percentage of GDP occurred in 1981—from 20.9 percent in 1980 to 27.6 percent by 1981.[4]

Economists analysing the explosion of the Mexican foreign debt between 1979 and 1982 generally agree that external economic shocks interacted with internal ones making the economic crisis of 1982 particularly severe. The explicit decision by the state to continue the expansionist strategy in the face of increasing interest rates and falling commodity prices, and the adverse reaction of the private sector to the effects of this decision, severely deepened the crisis. Indeed, it has been demonstrated that the effect of external shocks averaged less than 30 percent of the higher-than-trend indebtedness between 1979 and 1981.[5] Heavy government borrowing in 1981, especially short-term borrowing, was made necessary in part by the continued growth of government spending and heavy importing for the completion of investment projects. Total public expenditure represented 42.4 percent of GDP by 1981.[6] That same year the public-sector deficit as a percentage of GDP jumped to 14.7 percent from 7.4 percent in 1980.[7] But of even greater importance in deepening the crisis, especially after 1981, was the loss of confidence of the private business sector and consequent capital flight. This, it has been demonstrated, was the most important internal shock, accounting for on average slightly less than one-half of the internal debt-inducing effects between 1979 and 1981.[8]

The following section begins our analysis of the explosion of the Mexican debt after 1980 by examining private-sector

---

3 See Appendix Table 2.4.
4 See Appendix Table 2.2.
5 Leopoldo Solís and Ernesto Zedillo, 'The Foreign Debt of Mexico,' p. 270.
6 See Appendix Table 3.1.
7 Ibid.
8 These figures have been calculated from Leopoldo Solís and Ernesto Zedillo, 'The Foreign Debt of Mexico,' Table 10.5, p. 267. Quasi-populists within the bureaucracy argued that the balance of payments problem could have been alleviated by a strict policy of protection and by measures to control the outflow of capital.

objectives and the relationship between the state and this sector. It was the government's inability to maintain business confidence that precipitated the massive outflow of capital in 1981–1982 which severely deepened the crisis.

The State and the Private Sector Under López Portillo

Historically, the relationship between the Mexican state and the private sector has been fraught with periods of intense conflict. Entrepreneur–state conflicts have accelerated in recent years as the business sector has become ever more cohesive in ideology and organization. The old distinction between small and medium industrialists who were supportive of the state and of state intervention, and the big financial and industrial groups who were more hostile, has become less and less valid since 1970. Since that date there has been an increasing homogenization of views on most issues.[9] But despite this general likemindedness of private-sector ideology and organization, factions of capital continued to differ on policy matters related to their specific interests.

During the administration of López Portillo the relationship between the state and the private sector—especially its most powerful faction—was a cordial one, at least until the economic situation began to deteriorate in the spring of 1981. Although the private sector complained about state intervention in the economy, criticisms of specific aspects of government policy did not become prevalent until after 1980. Indeed, the restoration of business confidence had been one of the primary objectives of López Portillo's administration following the economic crisis of the mid-1970s.

Shortly after taking power, members of the Office of Economic Advisers to the President were dispatched to hold talks with private-sector leaders so that the president could become more aware of their concerns. Ten days after taking office the administration established an 'alliance for production' with the private

---

9 Even that organization purportedly representing small and medium industrialists, Canacintra, became critical of growing state intervention. This change in attitude may be attributable to the influx of foreign firms into Canacintra's ranks.

sector. By signing ten separate agreements with the business community, the private sector promised to make investments that would create 800,000 jobs, in return for the government's commitment to streamline both administrative procedures and provide financial and fiscal support. Generous incentives were provided for the reinvestment of profits, along with subsidies for the importation of machinery and equipment.[10] It was the biggest industrial financial groups that benefited the most from state largesse.[11] The ALFA group (one of the Monterrey group's holding companies) was a close collaborator of the López Portillo regime, investing in the government's priority areas and receiving various tax advantages and subsidies in return.[12] As a consequence ALFA and other privileged private-sector groups obtained high profits during the period. Average profits were increasing between 80 to 200 percent in the late 1970s and early 1980s.[13] Between 1974 and 1980 ALFA experienced an annual growth rate of 20 percent, and it more than doubled its number of enterprises.[14]

The 1978 multiple-banking legislation that stimulated the consolidation of the industrial–financial groups won the enthusiastic support of the most powerful faction of the private sector. Legislation passed in 1978, extending earlier legislation of 1970 and 1974, affirmed that specialized banking was obsolete and opened the way to multiple banking. Banking and credit legislation passed before 1970 had established various categories of

---

10 Salvador Cordero, 'Estado y burguesía en la decada de 1970,' in Jorge Alonso, coord., *El estado mexicano* (México, D.F.: Editorial Nueva Imagen, S.A., 1982).
11 María Elena Cardero and José Manuel Quijano, 'Expansion y estrangulamiento financiera, 1978–1981,' *Economía mexicana*, núm. 4 (1982): 190; Eduardo Jacobs and Wilson Perez Núñez, 'Las grandes empresas y el crecimiento acederado,' in ibid., p. 101.
12 On the growth of ALFA, see José Luis Manzo, 'Apéndice: El caso del grupo ALFA,' in José Manuel Quijano, coord., *La Banca: Pasado y presente* (México, D.F.: Centro de Investigación y Docenia Económicas, A.C., 1983). In 1979 it was reported that ALFA received 529,336 million pesos in tax advantages and subsidies. The amount increased to 1,600,295 million in 1980. See, *Razones*, núm. 39 (29 Junio 1981): 5. Between 1976 and 1980 ALFA received fiscal incentives worth 3,045,000 million pesos. *Unomásuno* (2 de Junio 1982): 1, 10.
13 Robert E. Looney, *Economic Policy Making in Mexico* (Durham, NC: Duke University Press Policy Studies, 1985), p. 119.
14 *Unomásuno* (2 de Junio 1982): 1, 10; María Elena Cardero and José M. Quijano, 'Expansión y estrangulamiento financiera, 1978–1982,' *Economía mexicana*, núm. 4 (1982): 186.

institutions—such as industrial banks, agricultural banks, mortgage banks, and deposit and savings banks—for the purpose of orienting resources to preferred areas. With the new legislation banks were now able to unite in one institution all of these activities.[15] This legislation also made it possible for Mexican banks to act in international capital markets. Although it had been originally assumed that the move toward multiple banking would contribute to financial deconcentration, it in fact had the opposite effect.

Increasing economic concentration had been a fact of Mexican economic life since the early 1960s. Powerful industrial and financial interests became linked through holding companies and connected to one of the major banks through bank ownership of shares and through financial ties. The financial group Serfín for example, one of the four largest private banks prior to the bank nationalization, was linked to the holding company known as VISA, one of the four subgroups of the powerful Monterrey group. VISA grouped together industrial enterprises involved in the production of beer, paper products, and electrical equipment. Grupo Financiera Banpaís was part of the holding company Vidriera (FIC), another subgroup of Monterrey. FIC grouped together enterprises involved in the manufacture and distribution of glass products. In other cases, the relations between banks and industrial enterprises were less formal.[16] From 1978 onward, these economic groups became increasingly concentrated with the biggest banks, Banamex and Bancomer, acquiring more and more industrial shares.[17]

The period 1978–1981 was one of high profits for banks, with the six largest banks capturing 85 percent of the profits.[18]

---

15 On the evolution of the Mexican banking system, see Javier Márquez, 'La banca en México, 1830–1983,' *El trimestre económico* 4, núm. 200 (Octubre–Diciembre 1983).

16 On this see Carlos Tello, *La nacionalización de la banca* (México, D.F.: Siglo XXI, 1984), pp. 37–38.

17 By 1982 Banamex was beginning to acquire some of the enterprises of the ALFA group, the powerful holding company for industrial enterprises involved in the steel industry. *Proceso*, núm. 306 (13 de Septiembre 1982): 14.

18 Carlos Tello, *La nacionalización de la banca*, p. 59. The six largest banks in Mexico were Bancomer, Banamex, Serfín, Grupo Internacional Nafinsa, Comermex, and Somex. Grupo Internacional Nafinsa and Somex were public financial groups. José Manuel Quijano, *México: Estado y banca privada*, 2d ed. (México, D.F.: Centro de Investigación y Docencia Económicas, A.C., 1982), p. 223.

Bancomer and Banamex increased their profits by 36 percent between 1980 and 1981, Comermex by 52 percent in the same period.[19] Indeed, the growth in strength of the financial and industrial groups appears to have occurred simultaneously with the formation of multiple banks and with the subsidies and tax advantages that aided the biggest enterprises.

The greater flexibility and consolidation of assets permitted by multiple banking would, bankers and the government believed, give national banks greater capacity in international markets. Mexican banks had been participating in the Euromarket from the early 1970s, but the new banking legislation further exhanced that penetration. The total number of loans conceded to Mexico from the Euromarket in which Mexican banks were participating increased from fifteen (between October 1978 and December 1979) to forty-four in 1980.[20] Mexican banks participated in syndicates that channeled loans toward the Mexican public sector, especially toward PEMEX.[21] The suspicion that the banking legislation of 1978 reflected the state's goal of using the national banking sector to direct more loans to the Mexican government may not be far from the truth.[22]

For most of the sexenio, then, the state and the most powerful financial and industrial groups were close allies. For the private sector the alliance with the state ensured high profits. For the state the alliance was a prerequisite for the pursuit of its economic strategy. At the same time, the border between the state and the private sector became increasingly blurred. Whereas in 1978 the state-run Nafinsa participated in seventy-six private enterprises, by 1982 this figure was eighty-six.[23] Somex, a state financial consortium among the six largest in the country, participated with ALFA and with multinational capital in the ownership of many companies. At the same time, private-sector participation

---

19 *Razones*, núm. 64 (14–27 de Junio 1982): 42.
20 María Elena Cardero, José Manuel Quijano, and José Luis Manzo, 'Cambios recientes en la organización bancaria y el caso de México,' in José Manuel Quijano, coord., *La banca: Pasado y presente*, p. 208.
21 Carlos Tello, *La nacionalización de la banca*, p. 122; José Manuel Quijano, *Estado y banca privada*, Table 2, p. 243.
22 Expressed in *Razones*, núm. 8 (21 de Abril–4 de Mayo 1980): 29.
23 María Elena Cardero and José Manuel Quijano, 'Expansión y estrangulamiento financiero, 1978–1981,' *Economía mexicana*, núm. 4 (1984): 185.

in state enterprises was common. Bancomer for example owned 461,798 shares in Nafinsa.[24]

It is clear that the most powerful faction of the private sector benefited handsomely from government measures to stimulate investment. These private industrial and financial interests joined forces with the government's petroleum expansionist strategy, producing for the petroleum and related industries, and helping to channel Euromarket loans to the public sector in support of the government's economic program. It is therefore not surprising that these financial and industrial interests were strong supporters of the government, at least until late 1980.

But from late 1980 and particularly through 1981 and 1982, the relationship between the state and the private sector, especially the biggest industrial–financial groups, became increasingly tense. As the economic implications of the expansionist petroleum strategy began to emerge, the private sector—with the exception of those interests tied immediately to the petroleum industry, such as petroleum contractors—began to withdraw support from the expansionist strategy. The increase in inflation and the unrest it engendered due to the loss of purchasing power made price controls on many commodities necessary. In early 1978 the private sector had forced the scrapping of price controls over a wide range of goods, and the government had subsequently attempted to hold down prices through informal agreements with the private sector. When this did not work, especially as inflation accelerated, price controls were reinstituted and the private sector clamored for their removal. But for Mexico's big banking interests, price controls were but a reflection of a far more important government failure: the failure to control inflation. Generally, inflation was blamed on the government for increasing its money supply, for allowing wages to rise, and for spending excessively. As the state continued to expand its activities, the biggest financial and industrial groups (represented by such organizations as the Association of Bankers) intensified their complaints about state intervention and the inefficiency of state enterprises. The growing overvaluation of the peso and the government's refusal to devalue was another important source of

24 *Proceso*, núm. 306 (13 de Septiembre 1982): 10.

tension.[25] The very rapid development of the petroleum industry had brought with it the liberalization of imports, a situation that threatened the survival certainly of the weakest indigenous firms. Industrialists also expressed concern about the impact of the overvalued peso on exports and urged measures to stimulate manufacturing exports.

When policy failed to respond to the private sector's concerns, capital flight accelerated. As we shall see in the following chapter the failure of the state to respond adequately to these private-sector concerns was related not only to fears of popular unrest but also to bureaucratic pressures. The following section examines the government's handling of the deepening economic crisis, which not only alienated the private sector but did little to satisfy growing popular unrest.

Crisis and Policy Response

The government developed three economic programs between mid-1981 and late 1982, as it tried desperately to deal with the economic crisis. The response of the state was not that of a cohesive and relatively autonomous organization with the vision to act in the long-term interests of capitalism and the capitalist class, but rather of a fragmented and weak state pulled and pushed by bureaucratic and private-sector clienteles and by its wish to maintain the political order.

The state's 'First Adjustment Program' was announced in June of 1981. It called for a reduction of the government's budget by 4 percent, a return to government industrial protectionism—reestablishing permits for over 80 percent of products whose importation had been liberalized—and measures to defend the peso. Despite this gesture, the government's refusal to allow the

---

25 The government's resistance to devaluation was very much political. A stable currency is very much tied in with Mexican national pride: in López Portillo's own words, 'The President who devalues is devalued.' On the causes of the 1976 devaluation and President Echeverría's pursuit of such a 'resistance strategy,' see Morris Clement and Louis Green, 'The Political Economy of Devaluation in Mexico,' *Inter-American Economic Affairs*, 32, no. 3 (Winter 1978).

deteriorating economic situation to interfere with its growth objective remained. The president took the decision not to apply brakes to the economy, and various government officials leapt to his defence, announcing that measures would not be taken that would contribute to unemployment.[26] As the president himself would explain in February of 1982, the decision had been made to pursue a strategy of 'responsible indebtedness'—that is, continued indebtedness with some effort to control government expenditure.[27] Faced with what he saw as a choice between slowing down economic growth and making adjustments coincident with the new reality, or using the state to stimulate further growth, the president chose the latter and—as he himself was later to admit—'lost control' of the situation.[28]

The practice of using PEMEX as a financial instrument of the state to obtain loans for other government departments and agencies—because of its credit worthiness—had begun as early as 1979. But the practice accelerated during 1981 and 1982 with the acquisition of a large short-term debt, especially during 1981. The boldness of the government in pursuing this strategy was matched only by that of the international banks who were more than willing to lend. Even when the oil glut was readily apparent by July 1981, the banks were oversubscribing Mexico.[29]

While public-sector spending and the deficit increased dramatically in 1981, the government received only $14 billion of an anticipated $20 billion in revenue as a result of the drop in petroleum prices.[30] By the end of 1981 the government's deficit was 100 percent higher than forecast.[31] Rather than reducing government expenditure by 4 percent for the remainder of the year as originally announced, the total actual federal expenditure was 18 percent above that originally authorized and 55 percent

26 See for example *Razones*, núm. 36 (14–17 de Mayo 1981).

27 *Proceso*, núm. 288 (10 de Mayo 1982): 19.

28 Ibid., núm. 289 (17 de Mayo 1982): 25.

29 Nicolas Asheshov, 'The Mexican Petrotrauma,' *The International Investor* (November 1981): 69.

30 David L. Wyman, 'The Mexican Political Economy: Problems and Prospects,' in David L. Wyman, ed., *Mexico's Economic Crisis: Challenges and Opportunities*, Monograph Series 12 (San Diego: University of California, 1983).

31 *Latin America Weekly Report* (December 4, 1981): 10.

above the expenditure for 1980.[32] Although PEMEX acquired the most debt in 1981—37.8 percent of the short-term debt and 27 percent of the long-term debt acquired by the public sector in 1981—its percentage of total public expenditure (19.6 percent) was down from that of 1980 (26.6 percent).[33] Bureaucratic opposition and international events had slowed the rate of expenditure in the petroleum sector. But expansion in other areas of the public bureaucracy forged ahead. In particular, parastates other than PEMEX were able to increase their expenditure at a faster rate between 1980 and 1981 than other areas of the public sector.[34]

As the economic situation deteriorated further, and with downward pressure on the national currency, the government began using foreign exchange reserves to defend the peso. In July 1981 and again in February 1982, the president stood firm against devaluation, declaring that he would 'defend the peso like a dog.' The government also began to bail out the private sector; it, like the public sector, had borrowed extensively on the international market and was by now running into severe liquidity problems. Most notably, ALFA began running into liquidity problems; in November of 1981 it was able to obtain a highly subsidized credit of 17 billion pesos from Banobras (Banco Nacional de Obras y Servicios, the state public-works bank). By August of 1981 the Monterrey group had already begun to modify its expansion plans, and massive layoffs of workers and employees had begun to occur. ALFA began to cancel investment projects and to divest itself of its companies. When the PRI's presidential candidate Miguel de la Madrid remarked that private enterprise could no longer be considered 'individual property,' the confidence of the private sector eroded further.[35]

In early 1982 PEMEX reduced the export price of Maya crude by $2 a barrel. In January 1982, following the threat of a general strike by the Confederation of Mexican Workers (CTM), a 34 percent increase was granted in the minimum wage. Powerful private-sector interests, which had declared their support for the proposed 4 percent reduction in government expenditure,

32 See Appendix Tables 3.2 and 3.3.
33 See Appendix Tables 2.5 and 3.4.
34 See Appendix Table 3.4.
35 *Proceso*, núm. 174 (1 de Febrero 1982): 28.

intensified their attacks on the government's expansionary program and pressed for devaluation, expressing their lack of confidence in the government's handling of the crisis. A massive capital flight occurred in late 1981 estimated at as high as \$2.5 billion (U.S.) during the first six weeks of that year.[36] By February 1982 the government had almost exhausted its foreign-exchange reserves in its efforts to defend the peso.

While business confidence deteriorated rapidly, the official labor movement remained generally supportive of the government. Both the president of the Labour Congress, and the secretary general of the CTM, Fidel Velásquez, declared worker support for the government's economic plan and their firm opposition to devaluation of the peso.[37]

The situation continued to unravel. Although the president had declared in early February that he would not devalue, the 'Second Adjustment Program'—announced on February 19—entailed a devaluation of 60 percent when the Central Bank withdrew support from the peso. The plan also called for a slowdown in economic growth and a reduction of 3 percent in government spending for 1982 that would not affect 'priority programs.'[38] The adjustment plan also included help to private- and public-sector enterprises that had debts in dollars. Indeed, the government absorbed much of the losses sustained by the private sector as a result of the devaluation. The secretary of natural resources and industrial development announced that the government would absorb up to 40 percent of the losses that companies suffered as a result of foreign-exchange transactions. But despite continued government largesse the private sector remained skeptical. In addition to the government's lack of commitment to cut back government expenditures, other elements of the program worried the private sector. Price controls on 5000 products had been decreed. And in mid-March, upward salary adjustments of 10, 20, and 30 percent were announced.[39] Although not entirely

---

36 *Latin America Weekly Report* (26 de Febrero 1982): 1.

37 *Unomásuno* (19 de Julio 1981): 1.

38 According to the Ministry of Budget and Planning. *Unomásuno* (10 de Marzo 1982): 11.

39 As a result of the devaluation, workers were demanding wage increases of 50 percent while the private sector would only agree to 9.2 percent. The failure of

happy with the situation, the official labor organizations were still willing to support the government's economic strategy. The refusal however of the private sector to implement the wage increases granted by the state was engendering increasing unrest. Most entrepreneurs resisted the new salary increases. And even those large enterprises who were paying the new higher salaries began to lay off workers.

As oil prices continued to slide, the regime embarked on its third adjustment plan. The 'Integral Program of Adjustment,' announced on April 20, was preceded by replacement of the secretary of finance and the head of the Central Bank, changes that signaled a turn toward more orthodox measures.[40] For the Mexican left, the April plan had all the trappings of an IMF program. It stipulated an 8 percent reduction in government spending, restrictions on the money supply, and revision of prices and tariffs in the public sector. The plan rejected exchange controls as unworkable, given the long border with the United States, and as producing further capital flight. But the initial orthodox nature of the program was mitigated by wage hikes of between 10 and 30 percent and subsidies to the private sector to maintain jobs. As in the other two adjustment plans little headway was made on reducing government spending. Public-sector expenditures continued to rise, with the public sector's deficit reaching 17.9 percent of GDP by 1982.[41]

Official pronouncements to the contrary, the situation was far from being under control. As will be seen in the next chapter, social tensions deepened as did the economic crisis. Capital flight continued. By June 1982 foreign banks began to renege on renewing loans that the Mexican government had been assured would be renewed. Renewal of the short-term loans that had been

---

capital and labor to reach an agreement resulted in the imposition of an agreement by the government.

40 In late March David Ibarra Muñoz, the secretary of finance, and Gustavo Romero Kolbeck, head of the Central Bank, were replaced by Jesús Silva Herzog and Miguel Mancera. Both were close to incoming President Miguel de la Madrid and were known fiscal conservatives. This change may also have been closely connected with the need to place key advisers of the incoming president in top positions to ensure continuity of policy, especially in the area of the budget.

41 See Appendix Table 3.1.

obtained in 1981 became increasingly difficult, and renewal periods became shorter and shorter. The IMF, which had sent a mission to Mexico in January, returned for further meetings in May and June. Negotiations with the IMF did not go well as Mexico resisted the IMF's insistence on a severe austerity program. Mexico then attempted, unsuccessfully, to negotiate with the private bankers itself. The situation now began to deteriorate rapidly. Having delayed the price increases called for in the earlier adjustment plan, the government on August 1 decreed price increases of 100 percent for bread and tortillas and 50 percent for gas. This measure precipitated financial panic and accelerated further the outflow of capital. By August of 1982 Mexico could pay only interest on its public foreign debt, while all payments on the private foreign debt had been suspended.

Measures implemented during August 1982 were contradictory in their purposes and impact and served to make more severe the economic crisis. On August 5, a second devaluation occurred when the peso was floated. Reversing earlier rejection of exchange controls, a system of dual exchange controls was implemented in an unsuccessful effort to control the outflow of capital. This measure merely exacerbated the problem by antagonizing the most powerful private-sector interests. Then, on August 12, in a further effort to stem the outflow of capital with the run on 'Mexidollar' accounts, the government announced that all dollar-denominated deposits in the Mexican banking system were to be paid in pesos at the free-exchange rate. This measure, rocking confidence in Mexico's financial institutions, was firmly resisted by the banking community. The president of the Association of Bankers declared that banks would continue to maintain accounts in foreign currencies and to pay depositors in foreign currencies.[42] Under intense public pressure, the government reversed itself on August 19. Exchange transactions were reinitiated with dollar-denominated deposits to be paid at 69.50 pesos per dollar, not at the free-market rate. This led to panic buying of American dollars, and North American banks reported that large quantities of dollars were being deposited in U.S. banks. The flight of capital during the last trimester of 1982

---

42 *Razones*, núm. 69 (23 de Agosto–3 de Septiembre 1982): 33.

was close to $1 billion (U.S. dollars). And throughout July and most of August, Mexico struggled to reach some sort of agreement with its creditors and with the IMF.

Conclusions

Although external factors played an important role in the 1982 crisis, internal factors were also of critical importance. Indeed it was the interaction between these external and internal factors that explains the depth of the 1982 crisis. The decline in petroleum prices and the increase in interest rates would not have had so devastating an impact had not Mexico embarked upon an import-intensive high-growth economic strategy. Certainly the effects of international events could have been mitigated had a decision been taken to slow down the economy in 1981 rather than continue its expansion. In other words, the acquisition of short-term debt at floating interest rates in 1981 produced a more serious crisis in 1982 than would otherwise have been the case. Of primary importance in the financial crisis of 1982 was the loss of the private sector's confidence and the massive flight of capital this loss produced. Although the state worked hard to restore and maintain the support of the private sector, and although state policy ensured the private sector high profits—benefiting especially the most powerful industrial–financial groups, traditionally antistatist—tension remained and increased as the state failed to take the measures recommended by the most powerful private-sector groups, particularly the financial community. The reaction of the private sector to the state's failure to deal decisively with the crisis in the manner deemed appropriate, indicates the very tenuous nature of the alliance between the state and the most powerful financial–industrial interests. Despite the banking sector's penetration of the state through the Ministry of Finance and the Central Bank, it was not able to alter the course of state policy to its liking. The state continued to adhere to an expansionary program supported by those bureaucratic and private-sector clienteles whose power and profits were closely tied to it. But although state policy did not respond to the disgruntled wishes of the most powerful

[125]

business interests, the state was clearly unable to shape the actions of those interests. In addition to being unable to stem the flight of capital, the state's contradictory and vacillating policy responses served to accelerate its outflow by further antagonizing the private sector and the middle class.

There is no question that the state's reluctance to embark upon a restrictive program was related to the possibility of a hostile reaction from organized labor. Indeed the government succeeded in maintaining the tacit—if not enthusiastic—support of organized labor during the crisis. But as we shall see in the following chapter, even more important was the need to satisfy bureaucratic clienteles.

The Mexican state, then, is a weak state heavily penetrated by capitalist interests—especially at certain points, such as state enterprises and state banking institutions. It does, however, retain an overriding state interest: a firm commitment to the survival of the political system. It also demonstrates the particularistic institutional interests of various institutions and departments of state and their clienteles. As a state with initiative but without coherence, it became increasingly less capable of taking measures to alleviate the crisis as that crisis deepened and as social tensions increased through 1982.

7

State Interests and the Politics of Patronage and Stabilization

Introduction

As we saw in the last chapter, the López Portillo administration's policy response to the softening of the petroleum market and rising interest rates deepened rather than alleviated the economic crisis. In particular, the decision to continue the pace of government borrowing and spending alienated the private sector and precipitated a massive outflow of capital, a situation that made necessary the acquisition of further debt. For the most part the government's policy response to the crisis did not coincide with the wishes of the private sector. Nor could it be said that state policy corresponded to the interests of the popular sector whose living standards most certainly deteriorated, especially after the decline in petroleum prices in 1981. Instead, specific political–bureaucratic interests—along with the general state interest in maintaining the continuity of the political system— were instrumental in patterning the direction of policy from the spring of 1981. This chapter examines the state interests that produced the decisions to continue the expansion of the economy and the debt after the spring of 1981, and to nationalize the banks in September of 1982. While the first of these decisions corresponded largely to the political–bureaucratic interest in lubricating the patronage system, the bank nationalization reflected the state's interest in maintaining legitimacy in the face of rising political unrest and a pending IMF stabilization program.

Political–Bureaucratic Factors in the Handling of the Crisis

One viewpoint blames the failure of the Mexican government to follow a consistent policy in its handling of the crisis on the contradictory pressures of conflicting bureaucratic positions. It has been suggested for example that the government's implementation of elements of the programs of both the quasi-populists and the neoliberals, while implementing neither program in its entirety, produced the inconsistency in economic policy described in the previous chapter.[1] On one hand, most notably, the neoliberals blamed the high growth rates and especially the rapid growth in public expenditure (seen by them as the main cause of the public debt and of the economic crisis) on the influence of the quasi-populists. This influence, it is argued, was exercised largely through the secretary of natural resources and industrial development, José Andrés de Oteyza. Other statist measures—such as price and exchange controls, in addition to wage increases granted to labor—were also blamed on the influence of the quasi-populists. The quasi-populists, on the other hand, argued that government policy failed because their program was not fully implemented due to neoliberal influence over such questions as trade liberalization and opposition to full exchange controls.

These charges of contradictory bureaucratic pressures do have some relevance. The president did vacillate between conflicting policy programs, especially during 1982. However, after the fall of petroleum prices in June of 1981, the decision taken not to slow down the economy and to continue foreign borrowing responded more to political and clientelistic pressures than to bureaucratic policy preferences. During the last two years of the López Portillo administration, two events central to the interest of the political bureaucracy were occurring: (1) the presidential succession struggle—that is, the choice of the PRI presidential candidate; and (2) the presidential and congressional elections to

---

1 See for example, Carlos Tello, *La nacionalización de la banca* (México, D.F.: Siglo XXI, 1984), p. 116; and Roberto G. Newell and Luis Rubio F., *Mexico's Dilemma: The Political Origins of the Economic Crisis* (Boulder, CO: Westview Press, 1984), p. 224. Officials interviewed by the author also voiced this view.

occur on July 1 of 1982. This context was critical in determining policy choices.

The presidential decision to continue borrowing and spending after the fall of petroleum prices in June 1981 had more to do with the momentum of the presidential succession struggle than with the influence of the quasi-populist faction. Faced with a drop in petroleum prices and government revenue, the Office of Economic Advisers presented a report to the president shortly thereafter outlining three alternatives: a sharp cutback in government expenditure, a moderate cutback, and the continuation of a high level of spending. The first alternative was the one recommended because the Office of Economic Advisers was aware of the always-intense pressure to go above budget during the fifth year of the sexenio, as presidential contenders attempt to garner support through patronage. It was expected that spending would be 20 percent higher than originally forecast. But President López Portillo chose to follow the middle course, as he did not wish to arouse opposition to the regime at a time when elections were pending. Attempting to avoid the usual burst in expenditures, however, he persuaded his secretaries to sign agreements that they would not go over budget.[2] This precaution could not, however, contain the intense pressure from all points within the bureaucracy to increase spending. Pressure was particularly intense from the parastates and from those 'political' departments dependent upon government expenditure to keep clienteles happy.[3] Indeed the president expects all cabinet secretaries and top governmental officials to look after their respective clienteles. It is especially important for those with presidential aspirations to demonstrate a basis of support obtained through effective manipulation of the patronage system. Hence, bureaucratic pressure for increased spending came from all of those cabinet secretaries who had presidential aspirations. In the

---

2 According to one informant, the president consulted the then secretary of budget and planning—a supposed fiscal conservative—Miguel de la Madrid, who pressed the president to take the moderate rather than the restrictive course. It appears that de la Madrid's presidential aspirations would have been adversely affected had he been forced to administer a restrictive budget.

3 The success of the parastates other than PEMEX in pushing expenditure beyond that of the previous year and beyond that originally authorized is demonstrated in Appendix Table 3.4.

[129]

case of the secretary of budget and planning, looking after one's clients meant acceding to expenditure requests emanating from all parts of the public bureaucracy. As one official interviewed in the course of this research put it:

> The viewpoint that public spending and borrowing ought to have been slowed down was expressed by economists within the government, but political necessities were much more compelling. . . . If you want to become President, you look after your clients.

In addition, the norms governing cabinet discussions that inhibit criticism of policy outside of one's policy area are reinforced during the later years of the succession struggle. Care must be taken in finding fault with the policies of other secretaries, as such judgments could be construed as criticism of the president, something to be avoided by those who have aspirations to succeed him. Furthermore, in the latter part of the presidential term, cabinet secretaries react to policy decisions in terms of who is the emerging presidential candidate, forming alliances that ensure political survival. In such a milieu voices critical of expansionism were not likely to come forward, and when they did they were not listened to.[4] Government officials were also able to obtain increases in expenditure by taking their requests directly to the president, thereby increasing the budget allocation beyond that originally authorized. This occurred with increasing frequency in the last two years of the sexenio and also contributed to the large budget overruns. Although this practice is technically illegal, the Institutional Revolutionary Party's (PRI) dominance of Congress and the control of PRI members through a system of cooptation and patronage assured that these extra expenditures were always approved after the fact, although not without considerable controversy in the press about the practice.

In short, the rhythm of expenditure and investment had to be kept up to lubricate Mexico's vast patronage machine. Once the presidential candidate was selected—the announcement was

---

4 Some of the officials interviewed suggested that the secretary of finance, David Ibarra Muñoz, a contender for the presidential candidacy, resigned having lost the president's confidence due to his views critical of rising expenditure, expanding debt, and his support for devaluation.

made on September 25, 1981—the election of July 1, 1982 became an increasingly important factor constraining the choice of policy. The captured interests, especially the middle-class and organized labor, had to be rallied behind the new PRI candidate. The transfer of power to the new president had to occur in an atmosphere of popular confidence in the PRI and in the political system. As the economic crisis deepened in mid-1982, this became an almost impossible task. Moreover the situation was made more difficult by the fact that Miguel de la Madrid, a technocrat with no previous electoral experience, seemed not to have the enthusiastic support of the 'politicos'—the old-time political leaders with ties to labor and peasant organizations. Indeed, rumor had it that de la Madrid's candidacy had been opposed by the labor movement. Believing that tough austerity measures would reflect negatively on the incoming PRI candidate (already somewhat under a cloud with the popular sectors due to his known fiscal conservatism), López Portillo sought to avoid such a program. Hence decisions such as the resistance to devaluation, expansion of public expenditure and debt, price controls, wage hikes, and subsidies to protect employment were designed to avoid the further alienation of the popular classes and the dissident left. These decisions, however, deeply antagonized the private sector. In view of the fact that the president had been advised that the slump in petroleum prices was short term, it is not surprising that given the political pressures to continue his expansionary program he chose to take this risk.

The economic policies of 1982 reflected the president's desperate attempt to contain the crisis. In this situation bureaucratic factions advocating competing policy orientations were able to influence the direction of policy at different times. With the failure of the first two adjustment plans for instance, the president became convinced of the efficacy of a more orthodox program; hence, he installed Jesús Silva Herzog and Miguel Mancera, known fiscal conservatives, as finance secretary and head of the Central Bank, respectively. When the situation continued to deteriorate, however, López Portillo became swayed by the more interventionist solutions of the quasi-populist faction: exchange controls, forced conversion of 'Mexidollars' to pesos, and finally the bank nationalization. But these policies also failed to contain the crisis and, indeed, exacerbated it due to the growing hostility of the middle classes and private sector.

Financial Rescue

By July of 1982 it was clear that Mexico was going to have to reach an agreement with the International Monetary Fund. The rumor that Mexico had been offering her petroleum as a guarantee for loans illustrated the gravity of the situation.[5] Indeed, by this time, private banks were insisting on an agreement with the IMF as a condition of further loans. While throughout 1982 powerful private-sector interests within Mexico were also agitating for an agreement with the IMF, within the political bureaucracy itself there was strong pressure to come to terms with the Fund. Beginning in July, a new team of the president-elect's had been working closely with IMF officials to work out a stabilization program. De la Madrid's team, along with officials in the Finance and Central Bank ministries, shared the IMF view that the principal cause of the economic crisis was government spending, disputing the official interpretation which laid blame entirely on external factors.

Meanwhile, however, the incumbent president's official position was that of strong resistance to an IMF agreement and an imposed stabilization program. As late as 1982 the director of external finance for the Ministry of Finance denied emphatically that talks with the IMF were being carried out, stating that an IMF stabilization program would not be necessary.[6] With the third adjustment plan, the government hoped to take sufficient measures to avoid the necessity of such an agreement.

In need of financing and unable as yet to come to an agreement with the IMF, Mexico obtained from the United States (on August 15, 1982), a loan for $1 billion (U.S.) in exchange for the future sale of an unspecified amount of petroleum for the U.S. Strategic Reserve, to be handed over during the next five years at a price $10 below the then average OPEC price of $34. The agreement

---

5 *Proceso*, núm. 299 (2 de Agosto 1982): 24; and núm. 288 (10 de Mayo 1982): 17.
6 *Razones*, núm. 68 (9–22 Agosto 1982): 19.

further stipulated that Mexico must reach an agreement with the IMF by mid-October. In effect the agreement meant that Mexico would be forced to violate one of the most nationalistic tenets of its petroleum program—not to sell any more than 50 percent of its petroleum exports to any one country. Not surprisingly the government attempted to keep this agreement from public knowledge. It was not mentioned in López Portillo's September report to the nation and did not become general public knowledge until the end of October.

On August 7 the finance secretary, Jesús Silva Herzog, made a formal request to the International Monetary Fund, and on August 17 he admitted publicly that the Mexican government was holding conversations with that organization. By the third week in August an IMF mission was in Mexico for more detailed negotiations. On August 18, it was reported that Mexico had reached an agreement in principal with the IMF so as to enable it to receive a $4 billion (U.S.) loan over the next three years.[7] A meeting between the finance secretary and representatives of Mexico's creditors took place in New York on August 20, and a loan of $500 million to $1 billion (U.S.) was agreed to for one year while a long-term solution could be worked out with the IMF. Mexico's creditor banks also agreed to a moratorium on the payments of principal on the debt (medium and short term) to give Mexico time to complete an agreement with the IMF.

The political fallout from the negotiations with creditors, especially the pending IMF agreement, was potentially very serious. Popular opinion was strongly opposed to an agreement with the International Monetary Fund, and yet there appeared to be no alternative. The petroleum expansionist strategy, despite some jobs created, had done little to calm political unrest, and indeed in recent years unrest appeared to be on the rise. Whereas the decision to continue the expansion of growth and debt responded largely to the immediate need to satisfy bureaucratic clienteles, pressures of a more general political nature became increasingly important as the crisis intensified and as the election and the transition of power approached. Hence, the president

---

7 Ibid., núm. 74 (1–14 Noviembre 1982): *Latin America Weekly Report* (August 29, 1982): 1.

now had to consider not just the competing policy pressures of opposing bureaucratic factions and the satisfaction of clienteles but also the popular basis of the regime.

Popular Unrest and the Bank Nationalization

As popular unrest increased in 1982, and as an unpopular IMF austerity program loomed on the horizon, the president was forced to distance himself from the finance sector's concern for liquidity and the achievement of an agreement with the IMF. Indeed, there was sufficient reason for concern about the popular basis of the regime. While the July 1 federal elections had seemingly rid the PRI of the stigma of absenteeism, the opposition parties had made notable inroads even in the face of large-scale electoral fraud. The PAN (the National Action Party), a right-wing party with business and middle-class support, made the greatest gains, achieving an unprecedented 14.08 percent of the popular vote. The PRI received 71.4 percent of the popular vote, down from its usual 90 percent.[8] Nor were all elements of the official Party particularly satisfied with the government's economic achievements. In May of 1982 the PRI's research institute (IEPES) called for structural changes it claimed were necessary due to the continuation of malnutrition, high unemployment, and high infant mortality among the urban and rural poor in the 1980s.[9]

Agitation from independent unions accelerated with the economic crisis. Criticism of the government's adjustment plans came particularly from those independent unions who had been critical of the government's expansionist petroleum strategy: from the nuclear workers' union and the university workers' union. By late 1981 opposition to the government's expansionist program and poor handling of the crisis were beginning to coalesce. On March 12, 1982, a dozen independent unions and leftist

---

8 Previously, only in 1946 and 1952 did the PRI's proportion of the votes cast fall below 80 percent. Roger Hansen, *The Politics of Mexican Development* (Baltimore: Johns Hopkins Press, 1980), p. 102.

9 *Unomásuno* (17 de Mayo 1982): 3.

political parties marched in Mexico City, calling for emergency measures to alleviate the increase in the cost of living.[10]

Between 1980 and 1982 unrest intensified in that area most neglected by public policy, the agricultural sector. Much of the agitation continued to occur in the petroleum zones as peasants demanded compensation for damaged and expropriated land. At the beginning of 1981, 1000 armed peasants blocked the petrochemical plant of Cactus and the petroleum fields of Reforma to back their demands for compensation; PEMEX was forced to suspend drilling and production for several days. The blockade was lifted when the government agreed to negotiate grievances. Another issue causing unrest in the petroleum zones was the extraction of union dues by the petroleum union from temporarily employed union workers.

While the government attempted to stage the appearance of concessions in order to quell unrest in the petroleum zones, the same cannot be said for its handling of land disputes. As agitation for land increased, so did repression. Land invasions accelerated and were dealt with harshly by authorities. In late 1981 seven peasants were killed when the police and the army used force to dislodge 8000 peasants from disputed lands in Sinaloa.[11] In July of 1981 three members of an independent peasant organization concerned with land claims were massacred by state police.[12] In early June of 1982 twenty-six peasants were killed in the municipality of Pantepec, Puebla, by gunmen sent by landowners; the peasants had occupied land that had been granted to them, though not yet officially handed over. Allegations that members of independent peasant organizations were being arrested and tortured by authorities were heard more and more in the press.[13] For the fifth time in 1982, a hundred campesinos were forcibly dislodged from land they had invaded in Ciudad Valles by order of the Ministry of Agrarian Reform; three were killed and thirty-five arrested in this incident.[14] Peasant organizations such as The

10 *Razones*, núm. 69 (23 de Agosto–3 de Septiembre 1982): 29.
11 *Latin American Weekly Report* (December 4, 1981): 12.
12 *Proceso*, núm. 248 (3 de Agosto 1981): 24.
13 *Unomásuno* (9 de Junio 1982, 16 de Junio 1982, 17 de Mayo 1982, and 17 de Mayo 1982).
14 Ibid. (11 de Junio 1982).

National Coordinating Plan of Ayala and The Independent Central of Agricultural Workers and Farmers protested the growing repression and government bias in favor of big capitalist agribusiness.[15]

It was within this context of rising social unrest and the inability of the state to manage the deepening economic crisis that the president announced the nationalization of the banks on September 1, 1982.[16] Dual exchange controls were announced also at this time: a preferential rate of fifty pesos per dollar and an ordinary rate of seventy pesos per dollar. At first glance the bank nationalization appears to have been a bold act demonstrating the relative autonomy of the Mexican state and its ability to contravene the wishes of powerful private-sector interests. But closer analysis reveals it as an act of desperation imposed by a faction of the political bureaucracy in charge of the state: the president and a group of advisers identified with the quasi-populist tendency.

The origin of the decision to nationalize the banks goes back to March of 1982. At that time the president asked for a report analyzing all of the economic policy options available to deal with speculation and capital flight.[17] One option analyzed in this document was nationalization of private-sector banks. Meetings with the president occurred on this question through March and April. As the economic situation deteriorated and as other policy courses met with failure, the frequency of meetings with the president accelerated, eventually convening practically on a daily basis by August. The group involved in these discussions was extremely small: the president; the former secretary of budget and planning, Carlos Tello; the secretary of natural resources and industrial development, José Andrés de Oteyza; and the president's son and deputy secretary of budget and planning, José Ramón López Portillo. Finance officials were not consulted about the decision because it was recognized that they would strongly oppose it and attempt to thwart its implementation. The presi-

---

15 Ibid. (25 de Mayo 1982).

16 Excluded from the nationalization was the American-owned Citibank and El Banco Obrero.

17 Much of the information given in the following paragraphs is taken from Carlos Tello's account of the decision. See Carlos Tello, *La nacionalización de la banca*, p. 9 ff.

dent did however consult a few people outside of his closest collaborators about the bank nationalization, all of whom apparently stressed its dangers.[18] Indeed, the president-elect, Miguel de la Madrid, was apparently not told about the decision until shortly preceding its official announcement, some reports suggest the day before. Not surprisingly he waited until the end of September before breaking his silence about the measure, finally declaring that the bank nationalization 'constituted an advance in the strengthening of the state as the 'rector' of national development.'[19]

For the quasi-populists, whose major spokesmen were Carlos Tello and José Andrés de Oteyza, economic arguments were paramount in the decision to nationalize the banks. For this faction the measure constituted the best means to stop the capital outflow and break the economic crisis. This argument likely had some considerable weight in the presidential decision (and was most probably believed by the economists making the policy recommendation); the economic argument, however, does not appear to have been the most compelling factor in the final decision. The political factor—the need to shore up the legitimacy if not the popularity of the regime in the midst of a deteriorating economic situation and rising social unrest—was the most important motivation behind the bank nationalization decision. Some of those *López Portillistas* who saw the decision as a poor one from an economic point of view (it did now stem the flow of capital nor alleviate the crisis), politically saw it as brilliant. In the words of one top official, 'The President was thinking of the interests of the political system. . . . He convinced us that it [the bank nationalization] was necessary for political reasons.' Although the president's September 1 speech referred to the flight of capital as a reason behind the decision to nationalize, there was also a clear attempt to link the measure to Mexico's revolutionary tradition, as shown by the President's assertion that—as a result of the measure—'the revolution is liberated from fear and is moving ahead.'[20] In addition the president apparently felt deeply

---

18 Carlos Tello, Ibid., p. 12.
19 *Proceso*, 308 (27 de Septiembre 1982): 22.
20 *Razones*, núm. 70 (6–19 Septiembre 1982): 21.

betrayed by the private sector upon which he had lavished so many benefits and advantages.

Politically, in the short term the decision appears to have had the effect intended. While it did nothing to avert the outflow of capital, the bank nationalization did much to rally popular support around the president. The decision responded to the old leftist desire to curb the power of the economically dominant banking sector. Heberto Castillo—leader of the Mexican Workers Party (PMT) and one of the regime's most vociferous opponents—who had been calling for the nationalization of the banks, apparently confessed to close friends the error of his past criticisms of the regime. All of the political parties with the exceptions of the PAN and the PDM (the Mexican Democratic Party) came out in support of the bank nationalization. The leading leftist party, the Unified Mexican Socialist Party (PSUM), declared that the nationalization opened up the 'possibility for an effective reordering of our economy.'[21] A political demonstration backing the nationalization two days after its announcement elicited strong support not only from the PRI and the official unions but also from the usually critical dissident left.

The reaction from the private sector was of course less than enthusiastic. (Its worries were shared by the Catholic church bishops as well.) The Monterrey group called for all commercial and industrial entrepreneurs to close their enterprises for one day in protest against the nationalization. Spokesmen for the group charged that the bank nationalization marked the transition of Mexico to a Cuban or Nicaraguan system.[22] Canacintra, the organization representing small and medium industrial firms, was less vehement in its opposition. Although opposed to the bank nationalization, Canacintra urged caution and argued against the temporary closure of businesses as such a measure would have been even more harmful than the bank nationalization itself.[23]

The bank nationalization did much to accelerate capital flight.[24]

---

21 Ibid., núm. 71 (20 de Septiembre–3 de Octubre 1982): 20.
22 *Proceso*, núm. 306 (13 de Septiembre 1982): 16.
23 Ibid., núm. 308 (27 de Septiembre 1982): 14.
24 Pascal Garcia-Alba and Jaime Serra-Puche, *Financial Aspects of Macro-Economic Management in Mexico* (Tokyo: Institute of Developing Economies, No. 36,

And although the international banking community may have been relieved that the Mexican government was assuming the debts of the now nationalized banking sector, the nationalization made reaching an agreement with the IMF difficult. Now, as the quasi-populist faction clashed with the finance secretary, Jesús Silva Herzog, over the old question of restricting versus expanding the economy, negotiations stalled with the IMF over Mexico's resistance to tough policies that would worsen unemployment. The quasi-populist faction had momentarily gained a position of decisive political influence at a time when the president was desperate for a way out of Mexico's deepening economic crisis. The IMF, impressed neither with the bank nationalization nor exchange controls, returned to Washington at the beginning of September. It made another attempt to resume negotiations at the end of the month.

The nationalization of the banks cannot be seen as signaling a restructuring of peripheral capitalism, nor of 'saving the capitalist class.'[25] The bank nationalization was the dying reflex of an about-to-be-replaced faction of the political bureaucracy. The measure reflected only the momentary relative autonomy of the state. For a brief period a faction of the political bureaucracy achieved autonomy from Mexico's powerful industrial–financial interests. Indeed, almost as soon as the nationalization was decreed, measures were taken to help restore the old equilibrium, as the political–bureaucratic faction linked to big industrial–financial interests strove to reassert itself. The financial sector within the state ensured that major changes were not made in the management of the nationalized banking system. Banks were largely left to function with their existing management. Only bank presidents were replaced.[26] The new appointments were of fiscal conservatives, figures very acceptable to the

1984), p. 49; Diane Stewart, 'Nationalization of the Banking Sector and Its Consequences,' in George Philip, ed., *Politics in Mexico* (London: Croom Helm, 1985), p. 138.

25 As suggested by Jesús S. Augustín Velasco, *Impacts of Mexican Oil Policy on Economic and Political Development*, (Lexington, MA: D. C. Heath, 1983), p. 38; and Wayne Oslo, 'Crisis and Change in Mexico's Political Economy,' *Latin American Perspectives* 12, no. 2 (1985): 20.

26 Timothy Hayman, 'Chronicle of a Financial Crisis: Mexico 1976–1982,' *Caribbean Review* 12, no. 1 (Winter 1983): 37.

business community. Former Finance Secretary David Ibarra Muñoz, for example, was appointed head of Banamex. And although the nationalization expanded state control of the economy to 80 percent—due to the fact that the banks held shares in industrial enterprises—the outgoing government of López Portillo announced the reprivatization of these industrial enterprises, a measure opposed by the Labor Congress.[27] The popularity of the bank nationalization apparently prevented complete reprivatization, although that was the policy preferred by many political bureaucrats within the Ministry of Finance and the Central Bank. But the new regime of Miguel de la Madrid announced almost immediately that 34 percent of the nationalized banking sector would be sold to private interests.[28] Moreover, in an effort to restore the confidence of the private-banking sector, bankers were compensated generously, some for more than their banks were worth. Indemnification paid for Bancomer, Banamex, Serfín, and Banreno for example was much higher than accounting or market value.[29] Under such circumstances, there was little possibility that the nationalized banking sector would become the financial instrument of a national development program. Those in charge of the nationalized banking sector were government bureaucrats with basically the same mind-set as those they had replaced.

The bank nationalization had attempted to recapture the old revolutionary populism that had been so consistently ignored during most of the sexenio. For a regime that had sold off Mexican resources at an ever-expanding rate, had formed a close alliance with big financial and industrial groups, and was about to conclude a strict stabilization agreement with the IMF, such a measure would give a much-needed shot in the arm to the regime's legitimacy. But the very depth of the crisis meant that the popular impact of the bank nationalization could only be short term. The National Front for the Defence of Salaries—a popular front integrating various left-wing organizations, includ-

---

27 *Proceso*, núm. 306 (13 de Septiembre 1982): 14.
28 The ley reglamentaria del servicio público de la banca y crédito of December 31, 1982.
29 Eduardo Villegas H. and Rosa M. A. Ortega O., *El sistema financiera mexicano* (México, D.F.: Editorial Laro, 1985), p. 18.

ing the PSUM and the Worker's Revolutionary Party (PRT)—demonstrated against government policy in late September, 1982. By mid-October the CTM was threatening a general strike if an agreement was not reached on its wage demands for a 50 percent increase.[30] By November speakers at a demonstration held by various left-wing organizations at the Zócalo, termed the bank nationalization a 'maneuver' by the political authorities.[31]

The agreement finally reached with the International Monetary Fund in November was a bitter pill, opening the country to further inequality. It called for a drastic reduction in public expenditures. The public-sector deficit as a percentage of GDP was to be reduced to 8.5 percent in 1983, to 5.5 percent in 1984, and to 3.5 percent in 1985.[32] The agreement also called for the liberalization of the economy, the elimination of new investment and employment plans, and increases in the prices of goods and services in the public sector.

Conclusions

Although state action was by no means the cause of Mexico's economic crisis, there is no question that state policy during the last two years of the administration of López Portillo worsened the situation. Pushed and pulled by the demands of private-sector and bureaucratic clienteles and by the rising social and political unrest, policy during the period was incoherent and vacillating. Although the state and the political bureaucracy, or factions of it, were still capable of initiative in the policy realm, their policies lacked the vision necessary to alleviate the crisis. While the bank nationalization did much in the short term to shore up the flagging legitimacy of the regime, social and political unrest continued through 1982. Moreover, the measure undoubtedly exacerbated the economic crisis over the long term by profoundly alienating the private sector and precipitating a massive capital outflow. In short the economic crisis—with its

---

30 A strike was averted when agreement was reached on a 30 percent increase.
31 *Razones*, núm. 74 (1–14 Noviembre 1982): 15.
32 'Carta de intención al fondo monetario internacional,' *El trimestre económico* 50 (2), núm. 98 (1983): 1130.

historical roots in the model of development pursued by the state since 1940—had been made even worse by a state policy that had to respond to competing bureaucratic and clientelistic pressures and to the increasing need to garner popular support as the economic crisis deepened.

8
Conclusion

This study has argued that the Mexican state, despite its ever-expanding intervention in the economy and its ability to act contrary to the wishes of the private sector, is a weak state. It is a state incapable of acting in the long-term interests of either capitalism or the capitalist class. A large and interventionist state does not necessarily demonstrate the presence of a strong state capable of a certain degree of autonomy and possessing coherence and vision in its actions. The notion of a 'state bourgeoisie' with an independent development project appears to have little relevance in the Mexican case. Private-sector interests have succeeded in permeating the state, sharing a similarity of attitudes with their bureaucratic allies.

As the creator of Mexican capitalism, the Mexican state was initially a strong state. However, while the state's role in the economy expanded, the private sector also underwent rapid growth and by the 1960s represented a serious constraint on state action. The growth of industry was reflected within the state by the rising importance of those departments, agencies, and parastates concerned with industrial development. Private-sector interests found ready access to the state through their bureaucratic allies, whose careers and institutional interests were strengthened by looking after the needs of their private-sector clienteles.

Since the mid-1950s the move toward a capital-intensive industrialization program, with its emphasis on high-technology projects, has given predominance to technocrats and to technocratic considerations in the formulation of policy. Mexico's old agrarista populism has virtually disappeared at the top levels of the political bureaucracy, while the regime's commitment to the popular classes, even in a symbolic sense, has gradually diminished. Although the old agrarista populism achieved a brief resurgence with the administration of Luis Echeverría, it was not represented among the top political leadership during the administration of President López Portillo.

The bottlenecks produced by the industrial model implemented by the state—and the changes in social structure induced by that model—have confined the political elite's policy choices within increasingly narrow limits. The tremendous growth in the private sector became an insurmountable obstacle to reforming Mexican capitalism along the lines of a 'shared-development' program. Faced with rising political unrest, however, the state sought a new strategy that could both restore business confidence and satisfy at least the captured labor movement, giving the masses of the population—through the achievement of rapid economic growth rates—at least the hope of a better life. Restoration of the flow of funds to government coffers was also of critical importance in order to ensure the workability of the state's cooptative mechanisms. These political necessities combined with the fortuitous coincidence of the rise in international oil prices and Mexico's discovery of substantial oil reserves, pushed its policymakers inexorably toward the petroleum export strategy. However, the political elite lost control of that strategy and was unable to utilize the opportunity in a manner conducive to stable economic growth. The petroleum export strategy followed its own logic, generating powerful vested interests that escaped central control.

In the Mexican case we cannot speak of any substantial degree of relative autonomy. Not if 'relative state autonomy' is taken to connote the ability to mediate class and intraclass conflict and to act in the long-term interests of capitalism and the capitalist class. Numerous examples exist of the state's inability to take measures that would have assured the smooth functioning of Mexican capitalism. Various efforts at tax reform were blocked by the private sector.[1] The state has been unable to pursue agrarian reform or gear public policy toward a substantial improvement of the agricultural sector. As many critics both within and outside of

---

[1] The tax reform carried out between 1978 and 1981 did represent, it has been suggested, important improvements in taxation. See Francisco Gil Díaz, 'The Incidence of Taxes in Mexico: A Before and After Comparison,' in Pedro Aspe and Paul E. Sigmund, eds., *The Political Economy of Income Distribution in Mexico* (New York: Holmes and Meier, 1984).

the government were well aware, the decision to follow a strategy of rapid petroleum exploitation and exportation contained many potential pitfalls. The Mexican state proved incapable of avoiding the most common of these dangers: neglect of the agricultural sector, heavy borrowing (especially after the softening of the petroleum market), and the wholesale pursuit of a capital-intensive industrialization program in the face of substantial unemployment and underemployment and accelerating rural–urban migration. Nor was the state capable of taking measures to alleviate the impact of the economic crisis and mitigate rising social tensions.

It is clear that a considerable degree of autonomy may occur between various agencies and departments of the Mexican state, which may escape tight central control. To some extent this situation may have contributed to political stability in the past insofar as it has been a means by which the government, through a network of patron–client relationships extending out into society, has absorbed and coopted political dissidents and potential dissidents. The Ministry of Agrarian Reform is an example of an attempt to use a department of the state to coopt peasant unrest. The Central Bank and the predominant role given to Mexican bankers prior to 1982 undoubtedly helped to assure the cooperation of the most powerful industrial–financial groups. On the other hand, the fact that PEMEX escaped central control as the petroleum strategy progressed, rendered the state unable to pursue a coherent economic program capable of mitigating the worst effects of the crisis.

It is apparent that considerable autonomy may occur between specific factions of the political bureaucracy and the propertied classes. The quasi-populist faction remained opposed to the economic program of the most powerful financial and industrial interests and succeeded in persuading the president to implement a significant portion of its own plan. The state may contravene the wishes of specific factions of capital—as occurred for example when the state resisted the orthodox stabilization program called for by the finance sector, or when it decided not to enter GATT. The possibility of relative autonomy however between the state as a whole and the propertied classes as a whole is far more problematic. When it occurs, not only must the international juncture be favorable but the period of relatively independent state action will be short lived. The operation of capitalism imposes constraints on state action insofar as the state must maintain business confidence if it is to maintain economic growth and popular support. And if we understand the state as a focus of class conflict, it is possible to see how these constraints operate within the state. At those junctures when relative autonomy appears possible, the resistance engendered by popular economic and political participation will be reflected in changes within the power structure of the state, as the overriding political goal of maintenance of the political order is paramount. That is, resistance to populist measures will be reflected in an intrabureaucratic struggle with the disaffected faction of state managers, forcing a readjustment of policy. This is what occurred in the later years of the Cárdenas period and again during Echeverría's attempt at shared development. It was also apparent following the nationalization of the banks in 1982 when that bureaucratic sector most closely allied with the bankers was able to ensure at least a partial reversal of the measure.

But although we argue the limited usefulness of a term such as relative autonomy, distinct state interests have an important impact on policy. There exists a general commitment to the continuity of the political system, and there exists specific institutional interests within the state. The interaction between state interests, societal pressures, and domestic and international economic circumstances may produce policies that satisfy no one and that exacerbate social tensions. The impact of the popular classes on state policy is felt through the political elite's commitment to the continuity of the political system. Obviously, in the years following the Mexican Revolution—when recently mobilized masses had greater political weight relative to the middle sectors and the business sector than is true today—political leaders had a far greater commitment to programs beneficial to the popular sectors. Now, the outside pressures acceded to are those from the private sector, from the middle class, and from the captured labor movement, as the political–bureaucratic technocratic elite becomes increasingly removed from its popular base. As the state has expanded its activities, institutional–bureaucratic interests reinforced by their clienteles have come to play a central role in the policymaking process.

The Mexican case demonstrates the complexity of state–private-sector relations. The struggle between the public and private sectors is a real one in the sense that while the public sector cannot control the behavior of the private sector, neither can the private sector pattern policy exactly to its liking. The private sector did not succeed in pushing state managers to greater economic orthodoxy after the drop in petroleum prices in 1981. Nor was it able to stop or to completely reverse the bank nationalization decision. However, there is no question that the private sector has been able to influence the state heavily through its penetration of the state at certain points. In the Mexican case, these points have been the Ministry of Finance, the Central Bank, and the parastates, particularly PEMEX. The penetration of the state by private-sector interests serves to reinforce institutional–bureaucratic infighting between those political bureaucrats having close ties to private-sector clienteles and those lacking them. This was seen, for example, in the various disputes between the quasi-populists and the expansionists and between the quasi-populists and the neoliberals.

Our analysis of the major policy debates in Mexico between 1976 and 1982 confirms those studies that have identified the increasingly technocratic nature of Mexico's political elite due to their training and lack of electoral experience. While industrialization brought to the fore those bureaucrats concerned with industrial activities, the petroleum export strategy further accelerated the rise to predominance of technocrats, especially those centered in PEMEX. Hence, during the policy debates of 1976–1982, there was no questioning of the capital-intensive industrialization model, no deep concern for the plight of small and ejidal agriculturalists, and no firm commitment to end social and economic inequality. It is questionable whether we can speak of a reformist faction of the state bureaucracy. In the Mexican case, this reformist faction comprised those political bureaucrats without close ties to private-sector clienteles. They did not, however, have ties with the popular classes, and on most counts they shared a basic agreement on fundamentals with the more private-sector oriented elements of the state bureaucracy. Reformist policies sprung from a commitment to the continuity of the political system, but one may question whether the Mexican political elite is any longer in touch with the requirements of that continuity. The populism that remains is a technocratic populism, concerned primarily with the protection of indigenous industry, the control of capital flows, and the expansion of employment in sectors such as construction and public works; this commitment does little to alleviate the plight of the nearly 50 percent underemployment in Mexico. Policy debates revolved around issues that could not affect the plight of the masses. Preoccupations with petroleum exploitation, the petrochemical industry, the capital-goods industry, or steel did not address the problems of urban underemployment, rural unemployment, or the crisis in the agricultural sector. When the agricultural question was addressed, the political elite agreed that it must be made 'more efficient' through infusions of capital, including multinational capital.

Mexico, it has been generally believed, stands out among Third World countries, and especially Latin American countries, for its ability to maintain social peace and political stability while pursuing an effective model of economic modernization—the so-called Mexican miracle. However, the Mexican state, it has been argued, is far weaker than generally assumed, while it has operated within an ever-narrowing range of choices. As petroleum prices declined, the range of choices became narrower still. Although state managers have a firm commitment to the continuity of the political system, they now have fewer options as to how that commitment will be achieved. The system has been bound together by a patron–client network that extends from the state into the broader society, lubricated by state spending. The system has been held together by a pragmatic exchange of benefits for support. We can expect in the coming years important changes in the nature of Mexican authoritarianism, particularly if petroleum prices do not rise. As the sexenio of López Portillo wore on, peasant and worker unrest during the period was increasingly dealt with by outright government repression. As Mexico's economic crisis continues and as the government's resources decline, adaptations to Mexico's authoritarian system may become especially important for those groups traditionally kept in line through patronage.[2]

The Mexican state, which demonstrated itself to be weak during 1976–1982, is likely to become more so. As well as having to contend with rising political unrest, the Mexican state more than ever is vulnerable to external pressures. The severity of Mexico's economic crisis has, of course, enormously increased the influence of the international banking community on policy choices. Attempts to alleviate the debt dilemma through 'debt for equity swaps' beginning in 1984 allows foreign investors to gain equity investment in a Mexican company by purchasing a portion of the company's debt. Such arrangements make it possible for foreign capital directly to penetrate nonstrategic parastates. These developments impact upon the distribution of power within the state and augur a further move away from the old populist formula that had been so successful in keeping the lid on social unrest.

We have argued that the Mexican state in its pursuit of the petroleum export strategy after 1976—and its handling of the economic crisis that began in the spring of 1981—acted neither in the interests of Mexican capitalism nor in the interests of the Mexican capitalist class. Nor did its program or handling of the crisis correspond to the interests of the popular sectors whose economic situation deteriorated, particularly after 1981. The pursuit of economic policies that deepen economic crisis and exacerbate social tensions has been characteristic of many Third World countries during the past decade. Rather than labeling such misguided state intervention as reflective of mismanagement or of errors in policy, a more fruitful approach may lie in an analysis of the state and state–societal relations and in an analysis of the underlying political logic of state action. Such an analysis may reveal, as in the Mexican case, a basically weak, fragmented state that, despite its extensive participation in the economy, finds itself captive of the economic and social contradictions of peripheral capitalism.

---

2 For a discussion of changes in the political system under de la Madrid and possible future scenarios, see Roderic A. Camp, ed., *Mexico's Political Stability: The Next Ten Years* (Boulder, CO: Westview Press, 1986).

Appendix

TABLE 1.1

Real GDP Growth, 1977–1983 (percentages)

1977	3.4
1978	8.1
1979	9.0
1980	8.3
1981	8.1
1982	−1.5

SOURCE: Clark W. Reynolds, 'Mexico's Economic Crisis and the United States: Toward a Rational Response,' in Donald L. Wyman, ed., *Mexico's Economic Crisis: Challenges and Opportunities*, Monograph Series 12 (La Jolla, CA: University of California, San Diego). p. 31.

TABLE 1.3

Mexico: Foreign Trade Indices (1975=100)

YEAR	EXPORT PRICE INDEX	IMPORT PRICE INDEX	TERMS OF TRADE INDEX
1976	100.1	101.0	99.0
1977	111.1	110.0	101.1
1978	114.0	124.0	92.0
1979	130.0	146.0	89.0
1980	159.0	166.0	96.0
1981	145.0	163.0	89.0

SOURCE: World Bank, *World Tables: The Third Edition, Vol. 1, Economic Data* (Washington, DC: Johns Hopkins University Press, 1983), p. 317.

[151]

TABLE 1.2

Petroleum and the Mexican Economy

	1976	1977	1978	1979	1980	1981	1982
Crude production average millions B/day	.8	1.0	1.3	1.5	1.9	2.3	2.8
Crude oil exports 1000's B/day	94	202	365	533	828	1,098	1,492.1
Petroleum & products % total value exports	16.8	22.4	29.7	43.8	67.4	74.4	73.6
% Total taxes paid by PEMEX	5.0	8.3	9.6	13.8	24.0	24.9	47.3
Food as % of value of all imports	4.0	9.2	8.4	6.9	8.2	9.4	13.1
Food as a % of value of all exports	35.8	33.7	24.8	20.2	10.1	10.4	9.6
Manufactures as a % of all exports	35.9	34.0	42.0	32.3	19.3	14.4	15.9
Consumer price index (1978 as base)	66.0	85.1	100.0	118.1	149.3	191.1	303.6

SOURCES: SPP, *La industria petrolera en México, 1980;* PEMEX, *Memorias de labores, 1980–1983,* Banco de México; *Informes annuales, 1976–1983;* Banamex, *Examen de la situación económica de México: México en cifras* (Agosto 1985).

TABLE 1.4

Mexico: Balance of Payments (millions of U.S. dollars)

	1977	1978	1979	1980	1981	1982
Current account balance	−1,596.4	−2,693.0	−4,870.5	−7,223.2	−12,544.3	−4,878.5
Total income	9,177.1	11,653.1	16,263.5	24,947.3	30,809.9	28,919.4
Merchandise exports	4,649.8	6,063.1	8,817.7	15,132.2	19,419.6	21,229.7
Other: services, tourism, etc.	4,672.1	5,590.0	7,445.8	9,815.1	11,390.2	7,687.7
Expenditure	10.773.5	14,346.1	21,134.0	32,170.6	43,354.1	33,797.9
Merchandise imports	5,704.5	7,917.5	11,979.7	18,832.3	23,929.6	14,347.0
Other: services, tourism, etc.	5,069.0	6,428.6	9,154.3	13,338.2	19,424.5	19.450.9
Capital account balance	2,276.0	3,254.1	4,533.3	11,948.3	21,859.6	8,573.9
Long-term capital (net)	4,271.3	4,689.0	4,591.0	6,835.2	11,696.2	10,368.1
Short-term capital (net)	1,995.3	1,434.9	57.8	5,113.1	10,163.4	−1,794.2
SDR's	—	—	70.0	73.5	69.6	0.0
errors & omissions	−22.5	−127.0	686.1	−3,647.5	−8,372.7	−8,361.6
Variation in Bank of Mexico Reserves	657.1	434.0	418.9	1,150.9	1,012.2	−4,666.2

SOURCE: Banamex, *Examen de la Situación Económica de México: Documento especial, México en cifras*, 1982, pp. 32–33; Banamex, *Examen de la situación económica de México: México en cifras* (Agosto 1985), p. 26.

TABLE 2.1

Distribution of Public and Private Foreign Debt

YEAR	PUBLIC DEBT (% OF TOTAL)	PRIVATE DEBT (% OF TOTAL)	TOTAL FOREIGN DEBT ($ MILLIONS U.S.)
1976	76.1	23.9	27,346.4
1977	77.8	22.2	30,633.7
1978	78.6	21.4	33,622.5
1979	73.9	26.1	40,257.2
1980	66.7	33.3	50,772.7
1981	70.4	29.6	74,056.0
1982	69.9	30.0	84,145.6

SOURCE: Leopoldo Solís and Ernesto Zedillo, 'The Foreign Debt of Mexico,' in Gordon W. Smith and John T. Cuddington, eds., *International Debt and the Developing Countries* (Washington, DC: The World Bank, 1985), Table 10.2, p. 261.

TABLE 2.2

Evolution of the Mexican Foreign Debt

YEAR	STOCK OF FOREIGN DEBT AS PERCENTAGE OF GDP	STOCK OF FOREIGN PUBLIC DEBT AS PERCENTAGE OF GDP
1976	32.6	24.9
1977	35.8	27.8
1978	32.7	25.7
1979	31.4	23.2
1980	31.3	20.9
1981	39.1	27.6
1982	43.1	29.8

SOURCE: Leopoldo Solís and Ernesto Zedillo, 'The Foreign Debt of Mexico,' in Gordon W. Smith and John T. Cuddington, eds., *International Debt and the Developing Countries* (Washington, DC: The World Bank, 1985), Table 10.2, p. 261.

TABLE 2.3

Relationship between the Servicing of the External Debt and Exports ($ millions of U.S.)

YEAR	1. EXPORTS	2. DEBT SERVICE	DEBT SERVICE RATIO (2:1)
1976	8,277	2,475	30
1977	9,177	3,837	42
1978	11,653	6,287	54
1979	16,283	10,174	62
1980	25,021	7,492	30
1981	30,810	9,543	31
1982	30,717	9,982	32

SOURCE: Miguel de la Madrid, *Primer informe de gobierno*, Anexo No. 1 (México, D.F.: 1983), p. 581.

TABLE 2.4

Long- and Short-term External Debt of the Public Sector (percentage of total)

YEAR	LONG TERM	SHORT TERM
1976	81.2	18.8
1977	88.0	11.9
1978	95.3	4.7
1979	95.1	4.9
1980	95.6	4.4
1981	79.7	20.3
1982	84.2	15.8

SOURCE: Miguel de la Madrid, *Primer informe de gobierno*, Anexo No. 1 (México, D.F.: 1983), p. 580.

TABLE 2.5

PEMEX Share of Public Debt (percentage)

YEAR	SHORT TERM	LONG TERM	TOTAL
1973	11.6	9.9	10.3
1974	3.2	10.8	9.3
1975	10.3	12.4	12.0
1976	10.7	11.5	11.3
1977	3.2	14.6	13.3
1978	—	17.3	16.5
1979	—	20.4	19.5
1980	10.5	23.1	22.6
1981	37.8	27.0	29.2
1982	33.9	25.3	27.1

SOURCE: Calculated from Miguel de la Madrid, *Primer informe de gobierno*, Anexo No. 1 (México, D.F.: 1983), pp. 577, 579, 580.

TABLE 3.1

Public Expenditures and Deficit as Percentage of GDP

YEAR	PUBLIC EXPENDITURE	PUBLIC-SECTOR DEFICIT
1976	33.6	9.9
1977	30.9	6.7
1978	32.2	6.7
1979	33.2	7.4
1980	35.6	7.4
1981	42.4	14.7
1982	48.9	17.9

SOURCE: Leopoldo Solís and Ernesto Zedillo, 'The Foreign Debt of Mexico,' Table 7, p. 271.

TABLE 3.2

Percentage Increase of Actual Total Public Expenditure over That Originally Authorized

YEAR	PERCENTAGE
1976	10.1
1977	1.8
1978	2.7
1979	13.2
1980	21.6
1981	18.4
1982	65.9

SOURCES: José López Portillo, *Tercer informe de gobierno*, 1 de Septiembre 1979 Anexo 1, Estadistico Historico (México, D.F.), pp. 60, 64, 65; Miguel de la Madrid, *Primer informe de gobierno: Sector politica economica*, Anexo No. 1 (México, D.F.), pp. 402–403, 418–419.

TABLE 3.3

Actual Public Expenditure Percentage Increase over Previous Year

YEAR	PERCENTAGE
1977	39.1
1978	29.3
1979	52.0
1980	55.1
1981	55.0
1982	79.3

SOURCES: José López Portillo, *Tercer informe de gobierno*, 1 de Septiembre 1979 (México, D.F.), pp. 60, 64, 65; Miguel de la Madrid, *Primer informe de gobierno: Sector politica economica*, Anexo No. 1 (México, D.F., 1983), pp. 402–403, 418–419.

[157]

TABLE 3.4

Federal Government's Originally Authorized and Actual Expenditures (Selected Administrative Units)

YEAR	OTHER PARASTATES		PEMEX		SOCIAL WELFARE		PUBLIC DEBT	
	AUTHORIZED	ACTUAL	AUTHORIZED	ACTUAL	AUTHORIZED	ACTUAL	AUTHORIZED	ACTUAL
1977	33.4	35.2	15.7	19.4	11.9	11.1	11.9	8.7
1978	34.5	34.8	20.3	20.6	11.0	11.1	12.4	12.7
1979	29.6	21.4	21.9	21.7	11.7	10.8	13.3	14.9
1980	9.8	14.9	32.9	26.6	11.8	11.3	13.5	11.1
1981	17.7	23.9	20.5	19.6	11.9	11.5	12.8	13.5
1982	19.3	19.7	13.9	19.0	13.3	8.8	17.9	27.4

NOTE: Social Welfare includes public education, health, labor and social welfare, and public works.

SOURCES: SPP, *Información sobre gasto público, 1970–1980* (México, D.F.: 1983); La Presidencia de la República, *Informes de gobierno*, (México, D.F.: 1977–1983).

Bibliography

Books

Allardt, Erik and Rokkan Stein (eds.), *Mass Politics*. New York: Free Press, 1970.

Alonso, Jorge (coord.). *El estado mexicano*, 2d ed. México, F.D.: Editorial Nueva Imagen, 1984.

Angeles, Luis. *Petróleo en México: Experiencias y perspectivas*. México, D.F.: Ediciones El Caballito, 1984.

Angeles, Luis. *Crisis y coyuntura de la economía mexicana*. México, D.F.: Ediciones El Caballito, 1979.

Aquilar M., Alonso et al. *Política Mexicana Sobre Inversiones Extranjeras*. México, D.F.: UNAM, 1977.

Aquilar M., Alonso and Fernando Carmona. *México: Riqueza y miseria*. México, D.F.: Editorial Nuestro Tiempo, S.A., 1972.

Aquilar Mora, Manuel. *El Bonapartismo mexicano*, Vol. 1, 2d ed. México, D.F.: Juan Pablos Editor, 1984.

Ashby, Joe B. *Organized Labour and the Mexican Revolution under Lázaro Cárdenas*. Chapel Hill: University of North Carolina Press, 1967.

Aspe, Pedro and Paul E. Sigmund. *The Political Economy of Income Distribution in Mexico*. New York: Holmes and Meier, 1984.

Barker,, Terry and Vladimiro Brailovsky (eds.) *Oil or Industry?* London: Academic Press, 1981.

Basáñez, Miguel, *La lucha por la hegemonía en México, 1968–1980*, 2d ed. México, D.F.: Siglo XXI, 1982.

Bennett, Robert L. *The Financial System and Economic Development: The Mexican Case*. Baltimore: Johns Hopkins University Press, 1965.

Benveniste, Guy. *Bureaucracy and National Planning: A Sociological Case Study in Mexico*. New York: Praeger, 1977.

Bermúdez, Antonio J. *The Mexican National Petroleum Industry*. Stanford, CA: Stanford University Press, 1963.

Booth, David and Bernard Sorj (eds.). *Military Reformism and Social Classes: The Peruvian Experience*. London: Macmillan, 1983.

Brandenburg, Frank. *The Making of Modern Mexico*. Englewood Cliffs, NJ: Prentice-Hall, 1964.

Brenner, Anita and George R. Leighton. *The Wind that Swept Mexico: The History of the Mexican Revolution, 1910–1942*. Austin: University of Texas Press, 1971.

Camp, Roderic A. (ed.). *Mexico's Political Stability: The Next Ten Years*. Boulder, CO: Westview Press, 1986.

Camp, Roderic A. *The Making of a Government*. Tucson: University of Arizona Press, 1984.

Camp, Roderic A. *Mexico's Leaders*. Tucson: University of Arizona Press, 1980.

Camp, Roderic A. *The Role of Economists in Policy Making: A Comparative Study of Mexico and the United States*. Tucson: University of Arizona Press, 1977.

Carlos, Manuel L. *Politics and Development in Rural Mexico*. New York: Praeger, 1974.

Carrada-Bravo, Francisco. *Oil, Money and the Mexican Economy: A Macroeconomic Analysis*. Boulder, CO, Westview Press, 1982.

Carillo Castro, Alejandro and Sergio García Ramírez. *Las empresas públicas en México*. México, D.F.: Miguel Angel Porrúa, 1983.

Castillo, Heberto and Rogelio Naranja. *Cuando el petróleo se acaba*. México, D.F.: Ediciones Océano, 1984.

Cline, Howard F. *Mexico: Revolution to Evolution, 1940–1960*. London: Oxford University Press, 1962.

Cline, Howard F. *The United States and Mexico*. Cambridge, MA: Harvard University Press, 1961.

Cockcroft, James D. *Mexico: Class Formation, Capital Accumulation and the State*. New York: Monthly Review Press, 1983.

Cockcroft, James D. *Intellectual Precursors of the Mexican Revolution, 1900–1913*. Austin: University of Texas Press, 1968.

Cockcroft, James D., André Gunder Frank and Dale L. Johnson. *Dependence and Underdevelopment*. New York: Doubleday, 1972.

Colegio de México (ed.). *Los Crises en el Sistema Politico Mexicano (1925–1977)*. México, D.F.: Centro de Estudios Internacionales, 1977.

Colegio de México (ed.). *La Vida Politíca en México, 1970–1973*. México, D.F.: Colegio de México, 1974.

Collier, David (ed.) *The New Authoritarianism in Latin America*. Princeton, NJ: Princeton University Press, 1979.

Conniff, Michael (ed.). *Latin American Populism in Comparative Perspective*. Albuquerque: University of New Mexico Press, 1982.

Cordera, Rolando and Carlos Tello. *La disequalidad en Mexico*. México, D.F.: Siglo XXI, 1984.

Cordera, Rolando and Carlos Tello. *México: La disputa por la nación*. México, D.F.: Siglo XXI, 1981.

Corredor, Jaime and Dalman Costa. *Petróleo, energía nuclear*. México, D.F.: Instituto de Capacitación Política, Partido Revolucionario Institucional, 1982.

Cosío Villegas, Daniel. *La sucesión presidencial*. México, D.F.: Editorial Joaquín Mortiz, 1975.

Cosío Villegas, Daniel. *El sistema político mexicano*. México, D.F.: Editorial Joaquín Mortiz, 1971.

Cumberland, Charles C. *Mexico: The Struggle for Modernity*. New York: Oxford University Press, 1968.

Cumberland, Charles C. *Mexican Revolution: Genesis under Madero*. Austin: University of Texas Press, 1952.

Deese, David A. and Joseph S. Nye (eds.). *Energy and Security*. Cambridge, MA: Ballinger, 1981.

Domínquez, Jorge I. (ed.). *Mexico's Political Economy*. Newbury Park, CA: Sage Publications, 1982.

Eckstein, Susan. *The Poverty of Revolution*. Princeton, NJ: Princeton University Press, 1977.

Ediciones Océano, S.A. *El desafío mexicano*. México, D.F.: Centro de Investigacion Cultural y Científica, A.C.; and Ediciones Océano, S.A., 1982.

Erb, Richard E. and Stanley R. Ross (eds.). *United States Relations with Mexico: Context and Content*. Washington DC: American Enterprise Institute for Public Policy Research, 1981.

Esteva, Gustavo. *The Struggle for Rural Mexico*. South Hadley, MA: Bergin and Garvey Publishers Inc., 1983.

Evans, Peter, Dietrich Rueschemeyer and Evelyne Huber Stephens. *State versus Markets in the World System*. Newbury Park, CA: Sage Publications, 1985.

Evans, Peter. *Dependent Development. The Alliance of Multinational, State and Local Capital in Brazil*. Princeton, NJ: Princeton University Press, 1979.

Fagen, Richard R. (ed.). *Capitalism and the State in U.S.–Latin American Relations*. Stanford, CA: Stanford University Press, 1981.

Fagen, Richard R. and William S. Tuohy. *Politics and Privilege in a Mexican City*. Stanford, CA: Stanford University Press, 1972.

Fann, K. T. and Donald C. Hodges (eds.), Readings in U.S. Imperialism. Boston, MA: Porter Sargent Publishing, 1971.

Fischer, Bernard, Egbert Gerken, and Ulrich Heimenz. *Growth, Employment and Trade in an Industrializing Economy: A Quantitative Analysis of Mexican Development Policies*. Tübingen, 1982. Germany: J. C. B. Mohr (Paul Siebeck), 1982.

Fitzgerald, E. V. K. *Patterns of Saving and Investment in Mexico*. Cambridge: Cambridge University Press, 1977.

Fitzgerald, E. V. K. *The State and Economic Development: Peru since 1968*. Cambridge: Cambridge University Press, 1976.

Fitzgerald, E. V. K., E. Floto, and A. D. Lehmann (eds.). *The State and Economic Development in Latin America*. Occasional Papers No. 1, Centre of Latin American Studies, Cambridge University. Cambridge: University Printing House, 1977.

Frank, André Gunder. *Crisis in the Third World*. New York: Holmes and Meier, 1981.

Frank, André Gunder. *Lumpenbourgeoisie, Lumpendevelopment*. New York: Monthly Review Press, 1972.

Frank, André Gunder. *Capitalism and Underdevelopment in Latin America*. New York: Modern Reader Paperbacks, 1969.

Freithaler, William O. *Mexico's Foreign Trade and Economic Development*. New York: Praeger, 1968.

Garcia-Alba, Pascal and Jaime Serra-Puche. *Financial Aspects of Macro-economic Management in Mexico*. Tokyo: Institute of Developing Economies, No. 36, 1984.

Glade, William P. and Charles W. Anderson. *The Political Economy of Mexico*. Madison: University of Wisconsin Press, 1968.

Glade, William P. and Stanley R. Ross (eds.). *Críticos constructivos del sistema político mexicano*. Austin: University of Texas Press, 1973.

Gonzaléz Casanova, Pablo. *Democracy in Mexico*. New York: Oxford University Press, 1970.

Goulbourne, Harry (ed.). *Politics and the State in the Third World*. London: Macmillan, 1979.

Goulet, Denis. *Mexico: Development Strategies for the Future*. London: University of Notre Dame, 1983.

Granados Chapa, Miguel Angel. *La banca nuestra de cada día*, 3d ed. México, D.F.: Ediciones Océano, 1984.

Grayson, George W. *The United States and Mexico: Patterns of Influence*. New York: Praeger, 1984.

Grayson, George W. *The Politics of Mexican Oil*. Pittsburgh: University of Pittsburgh Press, 1980.

Greenberg, Martin Harry. *Bureaucracy and Development: A Mexican Case Study*. Lexington, MA: D. C. Heath, 1970.

Greenwald, Joseph (ed.). *Latin America and World Economy: A Changing International Order*. Newbury Park, CA: Sage Publications, 1978.

Griffiths, Brian. *Mexican Monetary Policy and Economic Development*. New York: Praeger, 1972.

Grindle, Merilee S. (ed.). *Politics and Policy Implementation in the Third World*. Princeton, NJ: Princeton University Press, 1980.

Grindle, Merilee S. *Bureaucrats, Politicians and Peasants in Mexico*. Berkeley: University of California Press, 1977.

Hagen, Everett, E. *Planning Economic Development*. Homewood, IL: Richard D. Irwin, 1963.

Hamilton, Nora. *The Limits of State Autonomy: Post-Revolutionary Mexico*. Princeton, NJ: Princeton University Press, 1982.

Hampson, Fen Osler. *Fraught with Risk: The Political Economy of Petroleum Policies in Canada and Mexico*. Ph.D. diss., Harvard University, 1982.

Hansen, Roger D. *The Politics of Mexican Development*. Baltimore: Johns Hopkins University Press, 1980.

Hellman, Judith Adler. *Mexico in Crisis*, 2d ed. New York: Holmes and Meier, 1983.

Hewitt de Alcántara, Cynthia. *Modernizing Mexican Agriculture: Socio-Economic Implications of Technological Change, 1940–1970*. Geneva: UN Research Institute for Social Development, 1976.

Hewlett, Sylvia Ann and Richard S. Weinert (eds.). *Brazil and Mexico: Patterns of Late Development*. Philadelphia: Institute for the Study of Human Issues, 1982.

Hofstadter, Don (ed.). *Mexico, 1946–1973*. New York: Facts on File, 1974.

Johnson, Kenneth F. *Mexican Democracy: A Critical View*. New York: Praeger, 1978.

Kalecki, Michel (ed.). *Essays on Developing Countries*. Hassocks, Eng.: Harvester Press, 1976.

King, Timothy. *Mexico: Industrialization and Trade Policies since 1940*. London: Oxford University Press, 1970.

Koslow, Lawrence E. (ed.). *The Future of Mexico*. Tempe: Center for Latin American Studies, Arizona State University, 1981.

Ladman, Jerry R., Deborah J. Baldwin, and Elihu Bergman. *U.S.–Mexican Energy Relationships*. Toronto: D. C. Heath, 1981.

Leal, Juan Felipe. *México: Estado, bureaucracia y sindicatos*. México, D.F.: Ediciones El Caballito, 1975.

Lechner, Norbert (ed.). *Estado y Política en América Latina*. México, D.F.: Siglo XXI, 1981.

Levy, Daniel and Gabriel Székely. *Mexico: Paradoxes of Stability and Change*. Boulder, CO: Westview Press, 1982.

Looney, Robert E. *Economic Policymaking in Mexico: Factors Underlying the 1982 Crisis*. Durham, NC: Duke University Press Policy Studies, 1985.

Looney, Robert E. *Mexico's Economy: A Policy Analysis and Forecasts to 1990*. Boulder, CO: Westview Press, 1978.

Lustig, Nora (comp.). *Panorama y perspectivas de la economía mexicana*. México, D.F.: El Colegio de Mexico, 1980.

Manke, Richard B. *Mexican Oil and Natural Gas*. New York: Praeger, 1979.

Martínez Ríos, Jorge et al. *El perfil de México en 1980*, 7th ed., vol. 3. México, D.F.: Siglo XXI, 1980.

Martínez Nava, Juan M. *Conflicto estado empresarios*. México, D.F.: Editorial Nueva Imagen, 1984.

Megateli, Abderrahmane. *Investment Policies of National Oil Companies: A Comparative Study of Sonatrach, Nioc and PEMEX*. New York: Praeger, 1980.

Meyer, Michael C. and William L. Sherman. *The Course of Mexican History*. New York: Oxford University Press, 1979.

Miller, Robert Ryal. *Mexico: A History*. Norman: University of Oklahoma Press, 1985.

Millor, Manuel R. *Mexico's Oil: Catalyst for a New Relationship with the United States*. Boulder, CO: Westview Press, 1982.

Malloy, James M. (ed.) *Authoritarianism and Corporation in Latin America*. Pittsburgh: University of Pittsburgh Press, 1977.

Mosk, Stanford A. *Industrial Revolution in Mexico*. Berkeley: University of California Press, 1954.

Narvaez, Rúben. *La sucesión presidencial: Teoría y práctica del tapadismo*. México, D.F.: Instituto de Sociologia Politíca, A.C., 1981.

Needler, Martin C. *Mexican Politics: The Containment of Conflict*. New York: Praeger, 1982.

Needler, Martin C. *Politics and Society in Mexico*. Alberquerque: University of New Mexico Press, 1971.

Newell, G., Roberto and Luis Rubio F. *Mexico's Dilemma: The Political Origins of the Economic Crisis*. Boulder, CO: Westview Press, 1984.

Padgett, L. Vincent. *The Mexican Political System*. Boston: Houghton Mifflin, 1966 and 1976.

Parkes, Henry Bamford. *A History of Mexico*. London: Eyre and Spottiswoode, 1960.

Pérez López, Enrique et al. (eds.). *Mexico's Recent Economic Growth*. Austin: University of Texas Press, 1967.

Petras, James and Maurice Zeitlin (eds.). *Latin America: Reform or Revolution?* Greenwich, CT: Fawcett Publications, 1968.

Philip, George (ed.). *Politics in Mexico*. London: Croom Helm, 1985.

Poulantzas, Nicos. *Political Power and Social Class*. London: Sheed and Ward, 1973.

Poulson, Barry W. and T. Noel Osbourne (eds.). *U.S.–Mexico Economic Relations*. New York: Praeger, 1979.

Powell, J. Richard. *The Mexican Petroleum Industry, 1938–1950*. New York: Russell and Russell, 1972.

Purcell, Susan Kaufman. *Mexico–United States Relations*. New York: Praeger, 1981.

Purcell, Susan Kaufman. *The Mexican Profit-sharing Decision*. Berkeley: University of California Press, 1975.

Quijano, José Manuel (coord.). *La banca, pasado y presente (problemas financieros mexicanos)*. México, D.F.: Centro de Investigación y Docenia Económicas, A.C., 1983.

Quijano, José Manuel. *México: Estado y banca privada*, 2d ed. México, D.F.: Centro de Investigación y Docenia Económias, A.C., 1982.

Reyes Esparza, Ramiro, Enrique Olivares, Emilio Leyva, et. Ignacio Hernández G. *La burguesía mexicana*. 3d ed. México, D.F.: Editorial Nuestro Tiempo, 1978.

Reyna, José Luis and Richard S. Weinert (eds.). *Authoritarianism in Mexico*. Philadelphia: Institute for the Study of Human Issues, 1977.

Rondfelt, D. *Atencingo: The Politics of Agrarian Struggle in a Mexican Ejido*. Stanford, CA: Stanford University Press, 1973.

Saldívar, Américo. *Ideología y política del estado mexicano (1970–1976)*. México, D.F.: Siglo XXI, 1980.

Sanderson, Steven E. *The Transformation of Mexican Agriculture*. Princeton, NJ: Princeton University Press, 1986.

Sanderson, Steven E. *The Transformation of Mexican Agriculture*. Princeton, NJ: Princeton University Press, 1986.

Sanderson, Steven E. *Agrarian Populism and the Mexican State*. Berkeley: University of California Press, 1981.

Schafer, Robert J. *Mexico: Mutual Adjustment Planning*. New York: Syracuse University Press, 1966.

Scott, Robert E. *Mexican Government in Transition*. Urbana: University of Illinois Press, 1964.

Seligson, Mitchell A. and John A. Booth (eds.). *Political Participation in Latin America: Politics and the Poor*, Vol. II. New York: Holmes and Meier, 1979.

Smith, Gordon W. and John T. Cuddington (eds.) *International Debt and the Developing Countries*. Washington DC: World Bank, 1985.

Smith, Peter. *Labyrinths of Power*. Princeton, NJ: Princeton University Press, 1979.

Solís, Leopoldo. *La realidad económica mexicana: Retrovisión y perspectivas*, rev. ed. México, D.F.: Siglo XXI, 1981a.

Solís, Leopoldo. *Economic Policy Reform in Mexico*. New York: Pergamon, 1981b.

Stevens, Evelyn. *Protest and Response in Mexico*. Cambridge, MA: MIT Press, 1974.

Székely, Gabriel. *La economía política del petróleo en México, 1976–1982*. México, D.F.: El Colegio de México, 1983.

Tannenbaum, Frank. *Peace by Revolution: Mexico after 1910*. New York: Columbia University Press, 1966.

Tannenbaum, Frank. *Mexico: The Struggle for Peace and Bread*. New York: Alfred A. Knopf, 1950.

Tello, Carlos. *La nacionalización de la banca*. México, D.F.: Siglo XXI, 1984.

Tello, Carlos. *La política económica en México, 1970–1976*. México, D.F.: Siglo XXI, 1980.

Thorpe, Rosemary and Laurence Whitehead (eds.). *Inflation and Stabilization in Latin America*. London: Macmillan, 1979.

Toye, J. F. C. (ed.). *Taxation and Economic Development*. London: Frank Cass and Co., 1978.

Vanderwood, Paul J. *Disorder and Progress*. Lincoln: University of Nebraska Press, 1981.

Velasco, Jesús S. Agustín. *Impacts of Mexican Oil Policy on Economic and Political Development*. Lexington, MA: D. C. Heath, 1983.

Vernon, Raymond (ed.). *Public Policy and Private Enterprise in Mexico*. Cambridge, MA: Harvard University Press, 1964.

Vernon, Raymond. *The Dilemma of Mexico's Development*. Cambridge, MA: Harvard University Press, 1963.

Villegas H., Eduardo and Rosa M. A. Ortega O. *El sistema financiera mexicano*. México, D.F.: Editorial Laro, 1985.

Weyl, Nathanial and Sylvia. *The Reconquest of Mexico: The Years of Lázaro Cárdenas*. London: Oxford University Press, 1939.

Wilke, James W., Michael C. Meyer, and Edna Monzón de Wilkie (eds.). *Contemporary Mexico*. Berkeley: University of California Press, 1976.

Wilkie, James W. *The Mexican Revolution: Federal Expenditure and Social Change since 1910*. Berkeley: University of California Press, 1967.

Williams, Edward J. *The Rebirth of the Mexican Petroleum Industry*. Toronto: D. C. Heath, 1979.

Wionczek, Miguel S. (coord.). *Energía en México: Ensayos sobre el pasado y el presente*. México, D.F.: El Colegio de Mexico, 1982.

Wyman, Donald L. (ed.). *Mexico's Economic Crisis: Challenges and Opportunities*. Monograph Series 12. La Jolla, CA: University of California Center for Mexican Studies, San Diego, 1983.

Articles

Allub, Leopoldo and Marco A. Michel. 'Migración y estructura occupacional en una región petrolera.' *Revista mexicana de sociología* 44, núm. 1 (Enero–Marzo 1982).

Allub, Leopoldo and Marco A. Michel. 'Industria petrolera y cambio regional: El caso de tabasco.' *Cuadernos del centro de investigación para la integración social* México, D.F.), 1980.

Angeles, Luis. 'La política petrolera en México, 1976–1982.' *Cuadernos politicos*, núm. 32 (Abril–Junio 1982).

Asheshov, Nicolas. 'The Mexican Petrotrauma.' *The International Investor* (November 1981).

Atilio, Borón. 'New Forms of Capitalist State in Latin America.' *Race and Class* 20, no. 3 (Winter 1979).

Bailey, John J. 'Presidency, Bureaucracy and Administrative Reform in Reform.' *Inter-American Economic Affairs* 34, no. 1 (Summer 1980).

Bailey, John J. and Donna H. Roberts. 'Mexican Agricultural Policy.' *Current History* 82, no. 88 (December 1982).

Bamat, Thomas. 'Relative State Autonomy and Capitalism in Brazil and Peru.' *The Insurgent Sociologist* 1, no. 1 (Spring 1977).

Bennett, Douglas C. and Kenneth E. Sharpe. 'Agenda Setting and Bargaining Power: The Mexican State Versus Transnational Automobile Corporations.' *World Politics* 32, no. 1 (October 1979).

Berberoglu, Berch. 'State Capitalism and National Industrialization in Turkey.' *Development and Change* II, no. 1 (June 1980).

Berkstein, Samuel K. 'México: Estrategia petrolera y política exterior.' *Foro internacional* 16, núm. 1 (Julio–Septiembre 1980).

Bizzarro, Salvatore. 'Mexico's Government in Crisis.' *Current History* 72, no. 424, (February 1977).

Blair, Calvin P. 'Echeverría's Economic Policy.' *Current History* 72, no. 4, (February 1977).

Bloc, Fred. 'Beyond Relative Autonomy: State Managers as Historical Subjects.' *The Socialist Register* (1980).

Booth, John A. and Mitchell A. Seligson. 'The Political Culture of Authoritarianism in Mexico.' *Latin American Perspectives* 19, no. 1 (1984).

Bossio, Juan Carlos. 'La actual estrategia industrial mexicana.' *Revista mexicana de sociología* 43, núm. 2 (Abril–Junio 1981).

Bueno, Gerardo M. 'Desarrollo y petróleo: Las experiencia de los paises exportadores.' *El trimestre económico* 47, núm. 186 (Abril–Junio 1980).

Cabrera, Ignacio G. 'Acumulación de capital y política petrolera en México.' *Cuadernos politicos*, núm. 31 (Enero–Marzo 1982).

Cabrera, Ignacio. 'Crisis económica y estrategia petrolera.' *Cuadernos politicos*, núm. 28 (Abril–Junio 1981).

Cadero, María Elena and José Manuel Quijano. 'Expansión y estrangulamiento financiera, 1978–1982.' *Economía mexicana*, núm. 4 (1982).

Camp, Roderic A. 'Mexican Presidential Candidates: Changes and Portents for the Future.' *Polity* 26, no. 4 (Summer 1984).

Camp, Roderic A. 'The Political Technocrat in Mexico and the Survival of the Political System.' *Latin American Research Review* 20, no. 1 (1985).

Camp, Roderic A. 'A Reexamination of Political Leadership and Allocation of Federal Revenues in Mexico, 1934–1973.' *The Journal of Developing Areas* 10, no. 2 (January 1976).

Camp, Roderic A. 'The Middle Level Technocrat in Mexico.' *The Journal of Developing Areas* 6, no. 4 (July 1976).

Camp, Roderic A. 'The Cabinet and the Técnico in Mexico and the United States.' *Journal of Comparative Administration* 3, no. 2, (August 1971).

Canabal Cristiani, Beatriz. 'Política agraria: Crises y campesinado.' *Revista mexicana de sociología* 42, núm. 1 (Enero–Marzo 1981).

Canak, William L. 'The Peripheral State Debate: State Capitalist and Bureaucratic Authoritarian Regimes in Latin America.' *Latin American Research Review* 19, no. 1 (1984).

Cantu Segovia, Eloy, José Luis Medina Aguiar, and Agustín Basave Benitez. 'The Challenge of Managing Mexico: The Priorities of the 1982–88 Administration.' *Public Administration Review* 42, no. 5 (September–October 1982).

Cardoso, Fernando Henrique. 'Las Contradicciones del Desarrollo Associado.' *Desarrollo económico* 14, núm. 53 (Abril–Junio 1974).

Casar, José I. 'Ciclos económicos en la industria y substitución de importaciones, 1950–1980.' *Economía mexicana*, núm. 4 (1982).

Castillo, Heberto. 'Necesario plan de energéticos.' *El economista mexicano* 12, núm. 2 (Marzo–Abril 1978).

Clarke, Simon. 'Marxism, Sociology and Poulantzas' Theory of the State.' *Capital and Class*, no. 2 (Summer 1977).

Cleaves, Peter S. 'Mexican Politics: An End to the Crisis.' *Latin American Research Review* 16, no. 2 (1981).

Clement, Morris and Louis Green. 'The Political Economy of Devaluation in Mexico.' *Inter-American Economic Affairs* 32, no. 3 (Winter 1978).

Cockcroft, James D. 'Immiseration, Not Marginalization: The Case of Mexico.' *Latin American Perspectives* X, nos. 2 and 3 (Spring and Summer 1983).

Cockrane, James D. 'Mexico's "New Científicos": The Díaz Ordaz Cabinet.' *Inter-American Economic Affairs* 21, no. 1 (Summer 1967).

Colburn, Forrest D. 'Mexico's Financial Crisis.' *Latin American Research Review* 19, no. 2 (1984).

Coleman, Kenneth M. and Charles E. Davis. 'Preemptive Reform and the Mexican Working Class.' *Latin American Research Review* 18, no. 1 (1983).

Coleman, Kenneth M. and John Wanat. 'On Measuring Mexican Presidential Ideology Through Budgets: A Reappraisal of the Wilkie Approach.' *Latin American Research Review* 10, no. 1 (September 1975).

Conklin, John G. 'Elite Studies: The Case of the Mexican Presidency.' *Journal of Latin American Studies* 5, no. 2 (November 1973).

de la Peña, Sergio. 'Proletarian Power and State Monopoly Capitalism in Mexico.' *Latin American Perspectives* 9, no. 1 (Winter 1982).

de Olloqui, José Juan. 'Un enfoque bancario sobre la crisis mexicana de pagos en 1982.' *El trimestre económico*, 51(3), núm. 203 (Julio–Septiembre 1984).

de Riz, Liliana. 'Formas de estado y desarrolo del capitalismo en América Latina.' *Revista mexicana de sociología* 39, núm. 2 (Abril–Julio 1977).

Díaz Serrano, Jorge. 'La politica de petroleos mexicanos.' *El economista mexicana* 12, núm. 2 (Marzo–Abril 1978).

Dupuy, Alex and Barry Tuchil. 'Problems in the Theory of State Capitalism.' *Theory and Society* 8, no. 1 (July 1979).

Evans, Peter. 'After Dependency: Recent Studies of Class, State and Industrialization.' *Latin American Research Review* 20, no. 2 (1985).

Evans, Peter. 'Multinationals, State Owned Corporations and the Transformation of Imperialism: A Brazilian Case study.' *Economic Development and Cultural Change* 26, no. 1 (1977).

Fernandez Kelly, María Patricia. 'Dos Santos and Poulantzas on Fascism, Imperialism and the State.' *The Insurgent Sociologist* 7, no. 2 (Spring 1977).

Fitzgerald, E. V. K. 'The State and Capital Accumulation in Mexico.' *Journal of Latin American Studies* 10, no. 2 (November 1978).

Fitzgerald, E. V. K. 'Some Aspects of the Political Economy of the Latin American

State.' *Development and Change* 7, no. 2 (April 1976).

Gereffi, Gary and Peter Evans. 'Transnational Corporations, Dependent Development and State Policy in the Semi-Periphery: A Comparison of Brazil and Mexico.' *Latin American Research Review* 21, no. 3 (1981).

Goldfrank, Walter. 'World System, State Structure and the Onset of the Mexican Revolution.' *Politics and Society* 5, no. 4 (1975).

Gómez G., Octavio. 'Las empresas públicas en México: Desempeño reciente y relaciones con la política económica.' *El trimestre económica*, 49(2), núm. 194 (Abril–Junio 1982).

González Casanova, Pablo. 'La crisis del estado y la lucha por la democracia en América Latina.' *Revista mexicana de sociología* 42, núm. 2 (Abril–Junio 1981).

Grayson, George W. 'Oil and Politics in Mexico.' *Current History* 82, no. 488 (December 1983).

Gribomont, C. and M. Rimez. 'La política económica del gobierno de Luis Echeverría (1971–1976): Un primer ensayo de interpretación.' *El trimestre económico* 44(4), núm. 176 (Octubre–Diciembre).

Grimes, C. E. and Charles E. P. Simmons. 'Bureaucracy and Political Control in Mexico: Towards an Assessment.' *Public Administration Review* 29, no. 1 (January–February 1969).

Grindle, Merilee S. 'Patrons and Clients in the Bureaucracy: Career Networks in Mexico.' *Latin American Research Review* 12, no. 1 (1977).

Grindle, Merilee S. 'Power, Expertise and the Tecnico: Suggestions from a Mexican Case Study.' *The Journal of Politics* 39, no. 2 (May 1977).

Grindle, Merilee S. 'Policy Change in an Authoritarian Regime: Mexico under Echeverría.' *Journal of Inter-American Studies and World Affairs* 19, no. 4 (November 1977).

Gunder Frank, André. 'Mexico: The Janus Face of Twentieth Century Bourgeois Revolution.' *Monthly Review* 14, no. 7 (November 1962).

Hamilton, Nora. 'State–Class Alliances and Conflicts: Issues and Actors in the Mexican Economic Crisis.' *Latin American Perspectives* 11, no. 4 (Fall 1984).

Hamilton, Nora. 'The State and the National Bourgeoisie in Post-Revolutionary Mexico, 1920–1940.' *Latin American Perspectives* 9, no. 4 (Fall 1982).

Hamilton, Nora. 'Dependent Capitalism and the State: The Case of Mexico.' *Working Papers on the Capitalist State*, no. 3 (1975).

Handleman, Howard. 'The Politics of Labour Protest in Mexico.' *Journal of Interamerican Studies and World Affairs*, Vol. 18, no. 3, August 1976.

Harding, Timothy F. 'Dependency, Nationalism and the State in Latin America.' *Latin American Perspectives* 3, no. 4 (Fall 1976).

Hardy, Chandra. 'Mexico's Development Strategy for the 1980's.' *World Development* 10, no. 6 (June 1982).

Harris, Richard L. 'The Political Economy of Mexico in the Eighties.' *Latin American Perspectives* 9, no. 1 (Winter 1982).

Hayman, Timothy. 'Chronicle of a Financial Crisis: Mexico, 1976–1982.' *Caribbean Review* 12, no. 1 (1983).

Holloway, John and Sol Piciotto. 'Introduction: Towards a Materialist Theory of the State,' in John Holloway and Sol Piciotto (eds.), *State and Capital: A Marxist Debate*. Austin: University of Texas Press, 1979.

Holloway, John and Sol Piciotto. 'Capital, Crisis and the State.' *Capital and Class*, no. 2 (Summer 1977).

Ikonicoff, Moises. 'Teoría y estrategia del desarrollo: El papel del estado.' *El trimestre económico* 52(3), no. 207 (Julio–Septiembre 1985).

Imaz, Cecilia. 'La izquierda y la reforma política en México: Situación actual y perspectivas de la democracia.' *Revista mexicana de sociología* 42, núm. 3 (Junio–Septiembre 1981).

Jacobs, Eduardo and Wilson Perez Núñez. 'Los grandes empresas y el crecimiento acelerado.' *Economía mexicana*, núm. 4 (1982).

Jameson, Kenneth. 'An Intermediate Regime in Historical Context: The Case of Guyana.' *Development and Change* 11, no. 1 (January 1980).

Kaplan, Marcos. 'La teoria del estado en la America Latina contemporanea: El caso del Marxismo.' *El trimestre economico* 50(2), no. 198 (Abril–Junio 1983).

Kaplan, Marcos. 'El leviatán criollo: Estatismo y sociedad en la América Latina contemporánea.' *Revista mexicana de sociología* 40, núm. 3 (Julio–Septiembre 1978).

Lanfranco, Sam. 'Mexican Oil: Export-Led Development and Agricultural Neglect.' *Journal of Economic Development* 6, no. 1 (July 1981).

Langdon, Steven. 'The State and Capitalism in Kenya.' *Review of African Political Economy*, no. 8 (January–April 1977).

Lechner, Norbert. 'La crisis del estado en América Latina.' *Revista mexicana de sociología* 39, núm. 2 (Abril–Junio 1977).

Leys, Colin. 'Underdevelopment and Dependency: Critical Notes.' *Journal of Contemporary Asia* 7, no. 1 (1977).

Leys, Colin. 'The Overdeveloped Post-Colonial State: A reevaluation.' *Review of African Political Economy*, no. 5 (January–April 1976).

Márquez, Javier. 'La banca en México, 1830–1983.' *El trimestre económico* 4, núm. 200 (Octubre–Diciembre 1983).

Meyer, Lorenzo Cosío. 'El auge petrolero y las experiencias mexicanas disponsibles. Las problemas del pasado y la visión del futuro.' *Foro internacional* 18, núm. 72 (Abril–Junio 1978).

Miliband, Ralph. 'State Power and Class Interests.' *New Left Review*, no. 138 (March–April 1983).

Munck, Ronaldo. 'State Capital and Crisis in Brazil, 1929–1979.' *The Insurgent Sociologist* 9 (Spring 1980).

Niering, Frank E., Jr. 'Mexico: A New Force in World Oil. *The Petroleum Economist*, March 1979.

North, Lisa and David Raby. 'The Dynamics of Revolution and Counterrevolution: Mexico under Cárdenas, 1934–1940.' *LARU Studies* 11, no. 1 (October 1977).

Olson, Wayne. 'Crisis and Social Change in Mexico's Political Economy.' *Latin American Perspectives* 12, no. 3 (Summer 1985).

Orozco, Lourdes. 'Pemex y la crisis del petróleo.' *Cuadernos politicos*, núm. 15 (Enero–Marzo 1978).

Oszlak, Oscar. 'The Historical Formation of the Latin American State.' *Latin American Research Review* 16, no. 1 (1981).

Paoli Bolio, Francisco José. 'Petroleum and Political Change in Mexico.' *Latin American Perspectives* 9, no. 1 (Winter 1982).

Paré, Luisa. 'La política agropecuaria, 1976–1982.' *Cuadernos politicos*, núm. 33 (Julio–Septiembre 1982).

Patankar, Bharat and Gail Omvedt. 'The Bourgeois State in Post-Colonial Formations.' *The Insurgent Sociologist* 9, no. 4 ((Spring 1980).

Perez Sainz, J. P. 'Towards a Conceptualization of State Capitalism in the Periphery.' *The Insurgent Sociologist* 9, no. 4 (Spring 1980).

Petras, James. 'State Capitalism and the Third World.' *Development and Change* 8, no. 1 (January 1977).

Poitras, Guy E. 'Welfare Bureaucracy and Clientele Politics in Mexico.' *Administrative Science Quarterly* 18, no. 1 (March 1973).

Pompermayer, Malori J. 'The State and Dependent Development.' *Working Papers on the Kapitalist State*, no. 1 (1973).

Purcell, John F. H. and Susan Kaufman Purcell. 'Mexican Business and Public Policy,' in James M. Malloy (ed.), *Authoritarianism and Corporatism in Latin America*. Pittsburgh: University of Pittsburgh Press, 1977.

Purcell, Susan Kaufman. 'Business–Government Relations in Mexico: The Case of the Sugar Industry.' *Comparative Politics* 13 no. 2 (January 1981).

Purcell, Susan Kaufman. 'Decision Making in an Authoritarian Regime: Theoretical Implications from a Mexican Case Study.' *World Politics* 26, no. 1 (October 1973).

Purcell, Susan Kaufman and John F. H. Purcell. 'State and Society in Mexico: Must a Stable Polity Be Institutionalized?' *World Politics* 32, no. 2 (January 1980).

Raby, David L. 'Populism: A Marxist Analysis,' *McGill Studies in International Development*, no. 32. Montreal: McGill University.

Randall, Laura. 'Política Energética de México.' *Revista mexicana de sociología* 41, núm. 4 (1979).

Reyna, José Luis. 'Control político estabilidad y desarrollo en México.' *Cuadernos del CES*, no. 3. México, D.F.: El Colegio de México, 1974.

Reynolds, Clark W. 'Porque el "desarrollo estabilizador" de México fue en realidad destabilizador.' *El trimestre económico* 44, núm. 4 (Octubre–Diciembre 1977).

Rothstein, Frances. 'The Class Bases of Patron Relations.' *Latin American Perspectives* 6, no. 2 (Spring 1979).

Ruiz Durán, Clemente. 'Consideraciones sobre la petrolización de la economía mexicana.' *El economista mexicana* 14, núm. 3 (Mayo–Junio 1980).

Sanchez, A., Roberto 'The Oil Industry in Mexico.' *Third World Planning Review* 5, no. 1 (February 1983).

Sanderson, Steven E. 'Presidential Succession and Political Rationality in Mexico.' *World Politics* 35, no. 3 (April 1983).

Sanderson, Steven E. 'Political Tensions in the Mexican Party System.' *Current History* 82, no. 488 (December 1983).

Saul, John S. 'The Unsteady State: Uganda, Obote and General Amin.' *Review of African Political Economy*, no. 5 (January–April 1976).

Shapira, Yoram. 'Mexico: The Impact of the 1968 Student Protest on Echeverría's Reformism.' *Journal of Inter-American Studies and World Affairs* 19, no. 4 (November 1977).

Shaw, Timothy M. 'Zambia: Dependence and Underdevelopment.' *Canadian Journal of African Studies* 10, no. 1 (1976).

Shivji, Issa G. 'Capitalism Unlimited: Public Corporations in Partnership with Multinational Corporations.' *The African Review* 3, no. 3 (1973).

Skouras, Thanos. 'The "Intermediate Regime" and Industrialization.' *Development and Change* 9, no. 4 (October 1978).

Solís, Leopoldo. 'A Monetary Will-o-the-Wisp: Pursuit of Equity Through Deficit Spending.' World Employment Program Research Working Papers nos. 55 and 56, Joint Project with Research Program on Development Studies of the Woodrow Wilson School of Public and International Affairs. Princeton, NJ: Princeton University, March 1977.

Solís, Leopoldo. 'Mexican Economic Policy in the Post-War Period: The Views of Mexican Economists.' *The American Economic Review* 41, no. 3 (June 1971).

Spalding, Rose J. 'Welfare Policy Making: Theoretical Implications of a Mexican Case Study.' *Comparative Politics* 12, no. 4 (July 1980).

Stallings, Barbara and Richard Feinberg. 'Economic Policy and State Power: A Case Study of Chile under Allende.' World Papers on the Capitalist State, no. 3 (Spring 1975).

Story, Dale. 'Policy Cycles in Mexican Presidential Politics.' *Latin American Research Review* 20, no. 3 (1985).

Story, Dale. 'Industrial Elites in Mexico.' *Journal of Inter-American Studies and World Affairs* 25, no. 3 (August 1983).

Street, John H. 'Mexico's Development Dilemma.' *Current History* 82, no. 488 (December 1983).

Tuohy, William S. 'Centralism and Political Elite Behavior in Mexico,' in E. Thurber and Lawrence S. Graham (eds.), *Development Administration in Latin America*. Durham, NC: Duke University Press, 1973.

Tuohy, William and Daniel Rondfelt. 'Political Control and Recruitment of Middle Level Elites in Mexico: An Example from Agrarian Politics.' *Western Political Quarterly* 22, no. 2 (June 1969).

Turkok, Ben. 'Zambia's System of State Capitalism.' *Development and Change* 11, no. 3 (July 1980).

Turner, Teresa. 'Multinational Corporations and the Instability of the Nigerian State.' *Review of African Political Economy*, no. 5 (January–April 1976).

Velazquez Guzmán, María Guadalupe. 'Afectaciones petroleras en Tabasco: El movimiento del Pacto Ribereno.' *Revista mexicana de sociología* 44, núm. 1 (Enero–Marzo 1982).

Von Freyhold, Michaela. 'The Post-Colonial State and Its Tanzanian Version.' *Review of African Political Economy*, no. 8 (January–April 1977).

Wallerstein, Immanuel. 'Comments on the State and Dependent Development.' *Working Papers on the Kapitalist State*, no. 1 (1973).

Whitehead, Laurence. 'Mexico from Bust to Boom: A Political Evaluation of the 1976–1979 Stabilization Program.' *World Development* 8, no. 11 (November 1980).

Williams, Edward J. 'Petroleum Policy and Mexican Domestic Politics: Left Opposition, Regional Dissidence and Official Apostasy.' *The Energy Journal* 1, no. 3 (July 1980).

Wionczek, Miguel S. 'Algunas reflexiones sobre la futura política petrolera de México.' *Desarrollo económico* 23, núm. 89 (Abril–Junio 1983).

Yunez Naude, Antonio. 'Política petrolera y perspectivas de desarrollo de la economía mexicana: Un ensayo exploratorio.' *Foro internacional* 17, no. 4 (Abril–Junio 1978).

Zermeño, Sergio. 'De Echeverría a de la Madrid: Las clases altas y el estado mexicano en la batalla por la hegemonía,' Working Paper no. 118, Latin American Program. Washington DC: The Wilson Center, 1982.

Ziemann, W. and M. Lanzendörfer. 'The State in Peripheral Societies.' *The Socialist Register*, (London, 1977).

Newspapers/Periodicals

Commercio exterior
El día
Excélsior
Financial Times
Latin America Daily Report
Latin America Economic Report
Latin America Political Report
Latin America Weekly Report
New York Times
The Petroleum Economist
The Petroleum Times
Proceso
Razones
Tiempo
Unomásuno
Wall Street Journal

Government and Other Official Publications

Banamex, *Examen de la Situación Económica de México: Documento Especial, Mexico en Cifras* (México, D.F., 1982).

Banamex, *Examen de la Situación Económica de México:* México en Cifras (México, D.F., Agosto 1985).

Banco de Mexico, *Informes annuales*, 1976–1983 (México, D.F.).

Instituto Mexicano del Petróleo, *Plan integral para el desarrollo de la Industria Petrolera y Petroquímica Básica*, Período, 1973–1982. (México, D.F., 1972).

PEMEX, *Memorias de labores*, 1976–1982 (México, D.F.).

PEMEX, *Programas de operación*. 1967–1982 (México, D.F.).

La Presidencia de la República, Informes de Gobierno, 1977–1983 (México, D.F.).

Sepafin, *Plan nacional de desarrollo industrial, 1979–1982*. (México, D.F., 1979).

Sepafin, Comisión de Energéticos, *Programa de energía: Metas a 1900 y proyecciones al Año 2000* (México, D.F., 1980).

SPP, *Plan global de desarrollo, 1980–1982* (México, D.F., 1980).

SPP, *Cuadernos de divulgación* (México, D.F., various years).

SPP, 'Avances de Programa de Reforma Administriva (México, D.F., 1980).

SPP, Informe de labores, Período del 1 de Septiembre de 1976 al 31 de Agosto 1977 (México, D.F., 1978).

SPP, *La Industria Petrolera en México* (México, D.F., 1980).

SPP, *Programa de acción del sector pública, 1978–1982* (México, D.F., 1980).

U.S. Congressional Research Service, Library of Congress. *Mexico's Oil and Gas Policy: An Analysis.* Prepared for the Committee on Foreign Relations, United States Senate, and the Joint Economic Committee, Congress of the United States, Washington 1979.

U.S. Congressional Research Service, Library of Congress. *Project Interdependence: U.S. and World Energy Outlook Through 1990.* Summary report (Washington, DC: U.S. Government Printing Office, 1977).

U.S. Senate. *Geopolitics of Oil.* Hearings before the Committee on Energy and Natural Resources (Washington, DC: U.S. Government Printing Office, 1980).

World Bank, *World Tables: The Third Edition, Vol 1, Economic Data* (Washington, DC: Johns Hopkins University Press, 1983).

Index